Three
Comedies

Johann Nestroy

LITHOGRAPH BY JOSEF KRIEHUBER, 1839

Three
COMEDIES

by Johann Nestroy

A MAN FULL OF NOTHING · THE TALISMAN

LOVE AFFAIRS AND WEDDING BELLS

Translated (and fondly tampered with)
by Max Knight and Joseph Fabry

Foreword by Thornton Wilder

FREDERICK UNGAR PUBLISHING CO.
NEW YORK

1967

Picture credits: frontispiece, pp. 2 and 96, from the picture archives of the Österreichische National-bibliothek; p. 3, from Walter Gnaiger, Bregenz, Austria; p. 31, from Tiroler Landestheater, Innsbruck; p. 97, from Kurt Julius, Hannover, Germany; p. 177, from Helmut Baar, Vienna

FOREWORD

by Thornton Wilder

DURING the forties and fifties of the last century a famous actor-dramatist of Vienna was observed on a number of occasions, sitting alone in a café in the late afternoon. His manner became increasingly agitated. The hour of seven was approaching when the curtain must rise on his performance. He was trying in vain to call a waiter's attention, but shrank from rendering himself conspicuous. Finally a fellow guest would raise his voice and call out: "*Herr Ober*, can't you see that Herr von Nestroy wishes to pay his bill?" Yet an hour later this same shy actor, released from his torment at the café-table, would advance toward the audience with an introductory monologue' and song, expressing in his carriage and in the glances of his large brilliant eyes an unbounded insolence. The words he uttered and the pantomime that accompanied them attacked his public's most cherished illusions. Later,

v

when he rose to be manager of his company he never directed the productions himself. He lacked the courage to "correct" his fellow actors' performances. He arrived promptly at rehearsals, letter-perfect in his rôle. When scene-shifters bumped into him, it was Nestroy who tendered a deferential apology. There have been other examples of writers famous for aggressive and arrogant wit who have been mild and self-effacing in private conduct. Dr. Sigmund Freud, who delighted in Nestroy's work, has described wit as "the retaliation of the underdog."

Satire is aggressive. Cynicism is a devaluation of prevailing standards. What and whom was Nestroy attacking? Why did his audiences submit to—and even welcome—the large element in his writing and performance that was so obviously intended to render them uncomfortable?

Nestroy played in "second class" theaters—in the so-called *Vorstadt,* the suburbs that had recently been included in the new metropolis. The Viennese aristocracy and the "nicely" cultivated public attended the Burgtheater which offered long verse tragedies generally dealing with antiquity or the Middle Ages (occasionally these were by great hands; in *Der Talisman* Nestroy alludes to Grillparzer's *Ottokars Glück und Ende*). Nestroy's plays were felt to be "low." Though the majority of them picture the emerging newly wealthy middle classes, the parts he wrote for himself embody figures from a lower level of society—servants, apprentices, adventurers, and proletariat ne'er-do-wells.

Satire flourishes when society is passing through a state of transition, and transition contains elements of social and cultural revolt. The upward movement of a hitherto depressed stratum is accompanied by pretension, insecurity, and gaucherie. Two centuries earlier Molière was ridiculing these manifestations in *Le bourgeois gentilhomme, Les femmes savantes,* and other plays. Goldoni was constantly occupied with them and often at his best, as in *La casa nuova*. Beaumarchais laughed and shook his fist. It is not necessary to be a card-carrying Communist to observe that a large part of European literature during the last two centuries—tragic and comic—has been concerned with "class warfare." Numberless are the works, headed by the Don Juan and Faust legends, that derive a large part of their force from the seduction of a peasant girl by a man of privileged background. (Nestroy affords a powerful treatment of this situation in *Der Unbedeutende*.) Vienna was in social and political ferment. When finally the short-lived "March Revolution" of 1848 broke out in Austria, Nestroy himself manned the ramparts and wrote two comedies to celebrate the victory—disconcerting plays, however, for his satire was directed at both the oppressors and the liberators. For cynics there are no Utopias and little hope of meliorism. Satirists, like Swift, Voltaire, and Gogol, may declare their intention of bettering mankind, but one is left with an impression of their resigned acceptance of the doctrine of man's imperfectibility. We are often told that the object of comedy is to expose stupidity, restrain excess, unmask hypocrisy, and to chastise vice. Each of the masters returned repeatedly to certain targets: Aristophanes flayed his contemporaries' passion for political bungling (of little interest to Nestroy); Molière attacked medical quackery and religious hypocrisy (Nestroy has little to say about doctors and *never* alludes to religion). Most satirists, in so far as they are permitted—particularly those working in the late Middle Ages and early Renaissance—have exploited the scatological and the pornographic. Accounts of Nestroy's performances as an actor give the impression of having been accompanied by a constant play of obscene implications, yet scarcely a word of such matter can be read in the printed texts that have come down to us. This daring material appeared in Nestroy's rôle only and was conveyed by him in extempore improvisation and in glance, pause, and gesture. The censor threatened, critics voiced their outrage, a portion of the audience protested; but Nestroy could not restrain himself; his daemon drove him on. Two plays in this volume show very clearly where such material could have been inserted: Titus in *Der Talisman,* climbing up the social ladder, is the object of infatuation of a succession of women he despised and insulted; and the scurrilous Nebel in *Liebesgeschichten* (Moon in *Love Affairs and Wedding Bells*), pretending to make love to a rich and foolish spinster. In other words, Nestroy is not merely undermining the sentimental attitude to love, but the very instinctive drive itself. He depicts a sort of faun for whom one female is as acceptable as another.

The inner target of Nestroy's satire was the very ethos of Vienna's newly stabilized bourgeoisie: the pleasure-loving geniality, the famous *Gemütlichkeit.* In a play *Unverhofft,* written in the year following *Der Zerrissene* (*A Man Full of Nothing*), the character played by Nestroy himself says: "Only an unintelligent man can fail to see the omnipresent havoc underlying the apparently innocuous *Gemütlichkeit.*" What revolted Nestroy in his native city was not only the narrowness and coldness of heart that characterize all such milieux, but its predominant and stultifying characteristic of sentimental complacency—the smugness of small-town citizens living in a newly conscious metropolis. In the center of every play we find this Nestroy-figure, this disillusioned but clear-sighted outsider—often amoral, but never self-deluding—exposing the pretension of his audience, ridiculing their defenses, denouncing their sloth and the damage inflicted by their mindless subservience to outworn conventions.

Why did his public find enjoyment in this drastic devaluation of its self-image? Members of a parvenu social stratum are like adolescents, absorbedly self-conscious. They love to hear themselves discussed. They peer into mirrors. Even to hear themselves ridiculed becomes a "school of manners." But they soon tire of mere abuse; the darts must be accurate. The *vis comica* is always painful, but it is compelling in proportion to its truth. And Nestroy, aided by employing *their own dialect,* was unerringly actual. His wit cut to the quick. He walked a perilous tightrope and often suffered for his insolence. Enormously successful plays alternated with abject failures. (A number of those failures are now among the most admired of his works.) Finally, with the years his temper became milder. The rôles he wrote for himself in *Der Unbedeutende, Kampl,* and *Mein Freund* are still sharp-eyed and harsh spoken, but at heart they reveal themselves as merely kindly curmudgeons.

Of Nestroy's fifty major plays scholars have found only two which were not adaptations of novels or plays by others—the majority of them from the French. It is astonishing to observe with what fidelity he followed the plot structure of his foreign source. The invention of narrative patterns—"plotting"—did not interest him. Far more astonishing is the alteration he effected through the imposition of his own dialogue and characterization. Consider *Der Talisman,* for example: the young hero of *Bonaventure,* a vaudeville-comedy by Duperty and F. de Courcy, is the conventional young opportunist of French farce who reacts with banal surprise to the succession of wigs that circumstance offers him. In *Der Talisman,* Titus is the social pariah—victim of the prevailing prejudice against red hair—who avidly seizes each opportunity to advance himself. In Nestroy's hands the prejudice against red hair becomes a symbol of all the senseless ideas on which a *gemütlich* public nourishes itself. Titus is *aware* of it and, remaining in close rapport with the audience by means of asides, monologues, and songs, invokes their complicity in his heartless and even cruel advancement. (That is: in the dryness of heart that underlies the *Gemütlichkeit* and that snatches at any occasion for pleasure or wealth, no matter whom one tramples upon.)

Principally, however, Nestroy was forgiven his cynicism because of his extraordinary mastery of language. It is this that
has lead to the proverbial assumption in Vienna that "Nestroy
is untranslatable," by which is also meant untranslatable even
into German (an exaggeration that can be laid to local pride;
the distortion imposed by the dialect is less exotic than that
found in Hauptmann's Prussian and Silesian plays). Similarly
it is said of the great actor-dramatist of Naples today, Eduardo
de Filippo, that he is untranslatable even into Italian. Nestroy
avails himself of the German language's tendency to compound
nouns, forcing adjectival forms from polysyllabic (and poly-
glot) substantives, wrenching startling associations of ideas
from puns, and illuminating philosophical concepts by the use
of droll mixed metaphors. Most jokes lose their savor in translation and perish under dissection. The greater part of this
verbal acrobacy is entrusted to the Nestroy-figure and hence
derives a special fascination in the mouth of a character at the
bottom of society. Under a light screen of dialect *he* speaks a
highly sophisticated German; his is the only superior intelli-
gence in the play. The same pungency and force are found in
the utterances of Shakespeare's clowns—half beggars, the lowest of the servants, parasites at rich men's tables. Through
independence of *mind* the despised outsider elevates himself
to the rank of a penetrating judge of society and its mores.
Diogenes, the Cynic, is reported to have lived in a tub.

It has been a pleasure to learn that Mr. Max Knight and Mr.
Joseph Fabry, who know their Vienna well, have faced the
challenge of introducing Nestroy to English readers. It is, as
far as I have been able to discover, the first time that this
attempt has been made. I hope that this volume will find
many readers and that the authors will be encouraged to translate other plays of the great Austrian and that in time his work
will be presented in our theaters.

HALF A NESTROY

FOR A HALF-CENTURY AFTER NESTROY'S DEATH HIS
PLAYS REMAINED UNPERFORMED BECAUSE IT WAS
BELIEVED THAT WITHOUT NESTROY HIMSELF
ACTING IN THEM THEY WOULD HAVE NO APPEAL.
WHEN THE ATTEMPT TO REVIVE THEM WAS
MADE, IT SUCCEEDED.

FOR A CENTURY AFTER NESTROY'S DEATH HIS PLAYS
REMAINED UNTRANSLATED BECAUSE IT WAS BE-
LIEVED THAT WITHOUT THE VIENNESE DIALECT
THEY WOULD HAVE NO APPEAL. THE ATTEMPT
IS NOW MADE, NEVERTHELESS, IN THE CAUTIOUS
HOPE THAT, ALTHOUGH THE TRANSLATION
LOSES MUCH OF THE SPICE OF THE ORIGINAL,
THE ENGLISH-SPEAKING WORLD MAY WELCOME
GETTING TO KNOW AT LEAST HALF A NESTROY.

Contents

INTRODUCTION

During his lifetime, Johann Nestroy was the only actor to play the linguistic bravado parts he wrote for himself. But his repertory also included parts in comedies written by his contemporaries. A favorite was his Sansquartier, shown here, in Louis Angely's one-act farce *Zwölf Mädchen in Uniform.*

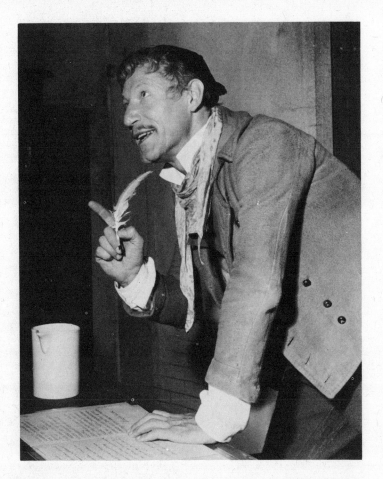

Today, every major theater in Austria and Germany has a "Nestroy player," but the mantle of Nestroy, the actor, has fallen on Josef Meinrad of the Burgtheater in Vienna. Meinrad, the present holder of the Iffland ring, the highest honor for an actor in the German-language area, is shown here as Herr von Lips in *A Man Full of Nothing* (*Der Zerrissene*).

Presenting
Johann Nestroy

JOHANN NESTROY, Vienna's philosopher-clown whom literary critics have called "the greatest German comedy writer"[1] and "the greatest, in fact, the only Austrian philosopher,"[2] is

[1] "Dennoch aber sagen wir, Umschau haltend im Bereich deutschen Schrifttums . . . , er sei der grösste deutsche Komödiendichter schlechthin. . . . So viel der Lessing der 'Minna' an erzieherischer Kraft, der Kleist des 'Amphytrion' und vielleicht Hofmannsthal in 'Christines Heimreise' an verschwiegenem Zauber, sie alle an betontem Abspruch voraus haben, um so viel übertrifft sie Nestroy an tiefem Witz und kühner Sorglosigkeit, durch unbekümmertes Schweifen vom volkstümlichsten Spass zur philosophischer Einsicht und an Vielfalt der Wirkungen. Hätte man von Lessing und Kleist und Hauptmann und Hofmannsthal nur ihre Komödien und kennte man Nestroy besser, so käme man nicht auf den Gedanken, sein Gesamtwerk niedriger zu stellen." Franz H. Mautner, *Johann Nestroy und seine Kunst* (Vienna: Otto Lorenz Verlag, 1937)
[2] Egon Friedell, *Das ist klassisch* (Vienna: Die Wiener Drucke, 1922)

5

hardly known outside the realm of the German tongue. Yet the one time that a Nestroy play was adapted by an American writer — Thornton Wilder — it became a triple success: on the stage, on the screen, and as a musical. But how many Americans know that *Hello, Dolly,* based on *The Matchmaker,* originated with somebody named Nestroy, who died in 1862?

Nestroy has been imprisoned in his language, the Viennese dialect. As Mr. Wilder has mentioned in his Foreword, Vienna's leading Nestroy specialist has declared Nestroy "untranslatable, not even translatable into German." [3]

But after World War II the Germans discovered Nestroy and are now claiming his works as among their own classics. He *has* been "translated into German," and thirty-five of his eighty-three plays have been staged and broadcast in Austria, Germany, and Switzerland. A two-volume selection from his works was published in Weimar in 1962; for that "translation" it was sufficient to explain some pithy Viennese expressions in a glossary — a method used even in Austrian editions for the benefit of Innsbruckers and Salzburgers, and even for the benefit of Viennese too far removed from Nestroy's nineteenth-century audience. Also in 1962, a thorough Nestroy biography was published in Munich. [4]

Isolated attempts to translate some of Nestroy's plays into cognate Germanic languages (Dutch, Swedish), and Thornton Wilder's *Matchmaker,* seem to demonstrate that Nestroy's humor, insight, and theatrical sense are strong enough to survive even if deprived of their charming, untranslatable dialect. To be sure, Wilder adapted, and did not translate, *Einen Jux will er sich machen;* perhaps the translations attempted here will inspire other Wilders.

Nestroy did not consider himself an important playwright.

[3] Hans Weigel, *Flucht vor der Grösse* (Vienna: Wollzeilen Verlag, 1960)
[4] Otto Forst de Battaglia, *Johann Nestroy* (Munich: Albert Langen-Georg Müller, 1962)

He was primarily an actor who could not find enough plays with parts suitable for his specific talents — so he wrote them himself. In a much-quoted passage spoken by one of his characters he says that his purpose is merely "to entertain" and to make a living, and that "to write funny stuff and reach out for laurels is a mixture of stupidity and arrogance — it's like somebody making a snowman and claiming to be a Michelangelo." [5]

Most contemporaries of Nestroy agreed with his self-evaluation, but some saw greatness behind the fool's mask. The writer Friedrich Schwarzenberg wrote: "In Nestroy lives a truly Shakespearean intellect, humor, and wit. He is a genuine poet of the people," and he predicted that Nestroy would be considered among "the noted dramatists of Germany." [6]

Still, his was a lonely voice. For thirty years after Nestroy's death most Austrians accepted his own judgment that his plays were merely fleeting entertainment. Besides, Nestroy had been such an overpoweringly funny comedian, and parts in his plays had been so much custom-made for himself, that the audience resigned itself to the sad fact that "Nestroy cannot be played without Nestroy." A generation grew up which no longer remembered the star of the eighteen-forties and -fifties. Works on German literature either mentioned him with scorn

[5] "G'fallen sollen meine Sachen, unterhalten, lachen sollen d'Leut, und mir soll die G'schicht a Geld tragen, dass ich auch lach', das is der ganze Zweck. G'spassige Sachen schreiben und nach dem Lorbeer trachten wollen, das is eine Mischung von Dummheit und Arroganz, das is grad so, als wie einer Zwetschgenkrampus' macht und gibt sich für einen Rivalen von Canova aus." (*Weder Lorbeerbaum noch Bettelstab*)

[6] "In Nestroy lebt ein wirklich Shakespearescher Geist, Humor und Witz; ein echter Volksdichter, und ich bin überzeugt, dass die Zukunft mein Urteil bestätigen und ihm einen ausgezeichneten Platz unter den dramatischen Notabilitäten Deutschlands anweisen wird." Friedrich Schwarzenberg: *Wanderbuch eines verabschiedeten Landknechts*. (The author, a traveler and writer, was a son of the victor over Napoleon in the Battle of the Nations at Leipzig, 1813.)

or not at all. Friedrich Hebbel called Nestroy's plays "poison-
ous and immoral farces," [7] perhaps with some feeling, because
Nestroy had used one of Hebbel's classical dramas as the
target of his wit. Literary scholars wrote about Nestroy's
"cynicism springing from . . . inborn vulgarity" [8] and about
the "unscrupulous manner in which he misused his not in-
considerable talent to flatter the most vulgar taste of the
masses." [9] Nestroy the popular comedian was dead, and
Nestroy the great satirical writer had not yet been discovered.
Only occasionally does one find a word of recognition. Ludwig
Speidel, the theater critic of Vienna's *Neue Freie Presse*,
wrote that Nestroy's "devastating irony could, on occasion,
rise to the heights of Jonathan Swift." [10]

Only twelve of Nestroy's plays were published (in individ-
ual volumes) during his lifetime.[11] When an enterprising
Viennese publisher, in the nineties, decided to publish a com-
prehensive collection of the plays, he had to search in the
cellars and attics of the two theaters in which Nestroy had

[7] "Friedrich Hebbel schrieb von den 'Augiasställen, die Nestroy hinter-
liess,' von seinen 'giftig-sittenlosen Possen.'" Weigel, *Flucht vor der
Grösse* (Vienna: Wollzeilen Verlag, 1960)

[8] "Nestroys Zynism entspringt . . . angeborener Gemeinheit . . . er ver-
mochte weder eine Handlung aufzubauen, noch wirkliche Gestalten zu
zeichnen". Richard M. Meyer, *Die deutsche Literatur des neunzehnten
Jahrhunderts* (Berlin: George Bondy, 1900)

[9] " . . . mit seinen in den besten Teilen von Raimund anhängigen
Volksstücken . . . missbrauchte Nestroy auf gewissenlose Weise sein nicht
unbedeutendes Talent, um dem gewöhnlichsten Geschmack des grossen
Publikums zu schmeicheln." Alfred Biese, *Deutsche Literaturgeschichte*,
vol. 2 (Munich: C. H. Beck'sche Verlagsbuchhandlung, Oskar Beck,
1907)

[10] "Sein vernichtender Hohn konnte sich momentan bis zu Swiftscher
Grösse steigern." Ludwig Speidel, *Kritische Schriften* (Zürich und Stutt-
gart: Artemis Verlag, 1963, quoting a newspaper article written in 1881)

[11] Paul Reiman, Introduction to *Nestroys Werke* (Weimar: Volksverlag,
1962)

worked, because most plays were available only in actors' well-thumbed working copies. Another source was Nestroy fans, such as Johannes Brahms, who had preserved some of his work.

The first real discovery of Nestroy's true stature, however, must be credited to the Viennese critic and gadfly, Karl Kraus, the uncompromising terror of the literary quack and a tireless seeker of the genuine. He published the belligerent and crusading *Die Fackel,* filled entirely with his own writings, and gave public readings of authors of whom he approved. He was feared by some Viennese writers and journalists whom he exposed, and worshipped by a large youthful following. On the fiftieth anniversary of Nestroy's death, in 1912, Kraus rented Vienna's largest concert hall and, to a standing-room-only crowd, read his re-evaluation of Nestroy, whom he called "the deepest satirical thinker the Germans have produced since Lichtenberg." [12] In later years Kraus repeatedly read from Nestroy's plays, often from Kraus's own adaptations. Vienna theaters started to produce the "farces with music" — first the theaters in the outlying districts, where lived the "plain people" for whom Nestroy had written, but eventually also the tradition-bound Burgtheater, the domain of the imperial court. The latter event may perhaps be comparable to a performance of *Hello, Dolly* at the Metropolitan. To the Viennese, this meant that Nestroy's plays had taken their place alongside the classics. The enthusiastic public and critical response to Nestroy's revival in Vienna was unique in the history of that theater-wise city. On the occasion of Nestroy's 150th birthday, *Der Monat,* Germany's leading international magazine for political and intellectual life, published an extensive evaluation of the playwright by Hans Weigel.[13] He pointed out that Nestroy was in immortal company when writing for "the peo-

[12] Karl Kraus, *Die Fackel* (Vienna, May 1912)
[13] Hans Weigel, "Johann Nestroy," *Der Monat* (Berlin, December 1951)

ple only," creating parts for certain actors, including himself, and doing this for no other reason than to entertain and make money. Shakespeare and Molière had done this, and so had Mozart and Verdi. World success had not been on their minds — they had not written in the expectation that centuries would listen to them. "Lucky Shakespeare and Molière and Nestroy," Weigel wrote, "lucky Mozart and Verdi, that you did not know that you were Shakespeare, Molière, Nestroy, Mozart, and Verdi! The burden of such knowledge might have drained your spirits and perhaps prevented your becoming Shakespeare, Molière, Nestroy, Mozart, and Verdi."

Today Vienna has its own Nestroy Theater which plays nothing but the works of the master.

An Unknown Classic

Johann Nepomuk Nestroy was born in 1801 in Vienna, the son of a lawyer whose ancestry can be traced to Polish Silesia, hence the "un-Austrian" name. Johann, too, studied law, but did not finish. He became an opera singer, first at the Vienna opera, then in the provinces, and later an actor in serious plays by Schiller, Grillparzer, and others. The story is told that his talent for comedy was discovered when he disliked one of the parts and tried to "throw" it by exaggerating it into a grotesque parody.[14] The story may be apocryphal, but it is in line with well-documented evidence of Nestroy's capacity to achieve devastatingly comical effects by gestures and intonations. His whole life was one long fight against the censor, to whom he had to submit his plays in advance and whom he outwitted by a raised eyebrow, a twitching lip, or a stress on a word, thus giving subtle and subversive meanings to words that looked harmless in print.

[14] Otto Rommel, *Johann Nestroy* (Vienna: Anton Schroll & Co., 1948)

In 1831, at the age of thirty, Nestroy returned from the provinces to his native Vienna. Theater life in the city was divided between the literary drama performed in the formal presentations of the Inner City and the popular shows performed in the outskirts. These two forms, which Shakespeare had skillfully united in his plays, were cultivated separately in Vienna. The serious literary drama, performed in classical German, was the fare for Vienna's aristocracy. But the masses went to their own theaters, which gave them what they wanted: raw comedies and tear jerkers in the heavy Viennese idiom, the Austrian versions of the commedia dell'arte. These plays had become stereotyped — fairy pieces, romantic stories, vulgar Hanswurst (clown) farces — but the crumbling of the class system and the emergence of a moneyed aristocracy broke up the stereotypes, a process in which Nestroy helped. He was not primarily a revolutionary — not so much a fighter for a brave new world as a ridiculer of the tradition-ridden old one. He brought to the Vienna theater the aggressive-pessimistic thrust of his satire, and a rebellious wit that passed from mouth to mouth — amusing but deadly darts against conformity.

A View of Man and His World

Nestroy's X-ray eyes saw through sham, pretense, and fraud, and exposed man's miserable motives. In all Nestroy plays the main character was written for himself, and speaks for himself. Buried in slapstick comedy lay his philosophy, his sober view of man: "Two wolves can meet without being afraid of each other, but two men meeting in a dark forest always will think, 'He is a robber.'"

Nestroy saw man as tossed about by a fate that remained completely unconcerned. In one of his early plays, when he was still using the traditional framework of the fairy piece (though he used it as a parody), Father Fate, resting on a cloud, is asked for help by his nephew Stellaris. Fate cuts short all explanations:

> FATE: I know everything. (*To himself*) I don't know a thing, but I'm much too lazy to listen. It's great to be Fate: one does nothing and gets credit for everything.
> STELLARIS: Then we may hope?
> FATE: Of course. Go ahead and hope! (*Sits down on his cloud and falls asleep again.*)

Nestroy soon discarded the framework of the world of magic and concentrated on man on earth, but fate still remains "a miserable ruler, Nero and Louis XIV wrapped in one." Man is tyrannized by fate as much as by a dictatorial king, but he rebels: "They say that a man's chances are dealt like a card from the deck of destiny — if I could find the cardsharp who dealt mine I'd club him one on the head."

Man's life is sweetened by love which, unfortunately, tends to degenerate into marriage. "Love is a string that ties hearts together, and marriage a rope that ties hands; the string can be broken, but the rope — never." His dim view of marriage may be the result of his own experience: he married very young, divorced his wife when he found her with a lover, and for the rest of his life he had one affair after another while living with a common-law wife whom he, as a Catholic, could not marry.

Nestroy lived in an era when one did not talk about sex, but he did not hide his opinion that sex, next to money and plain human cussedness, is man's greatest motivation. "In the drama of love, the first act is called longing, the second possession. And impatient youth will not stand for an intermission." But some of his most pointed barbs were saved for marriage: "Is there a better opportunity to make someone you hate unhappy than to marry him?" "Love is called happy if

it results in what is often the greatest mishap: marriage."
"Marriage is always a tragedy, because one of the partners
must die — or it doesn't end." Marriage, to Nestroy, was "a
mutual life annoyance company," which, however, did not
keep him from including one and, more often, several mar-
riages in the conventional happy endings of his plays. "I've
never found anything distasteful," he wrote, "in seeing someone else getting married."

The remnants of feudalism are still in evidence in Nestroy's
plays. The aristocrat, in his mansion, is the protector of the
people in the village and controls the local police. But the
newly rich man can now buy the mansion and the power,
and this, of course, is comedy. And Nestroy can pour forth his
irony against the rich, which censorship does not allow him
to do against the establishment, the aristocrats. All problems
are solved by money, often come by in the crudest form: a
sudden inheritance, an unforeseen treasure, an unexpected
gift. Nestroy himself ridicules his own use of unexpected
money to bring about happy endings: "Has it happened
again?" one of his main characters calls out just before the
last curtain. "It's incredible how many rich uncles and aunts
die every year so everything will end well!"

A Social Critic

Although Nestroy ridicules the rich, he is no social reformer.
He is a writer of the people and for the people, but not a par-
ticipant in the class war.[15] Class distinctions exist — between

---

[15] A selection of Nestroy plays, published in East Germany (Volksverlag
Weimar, 1962), attempts to present Nestroy as class conscious in the
Marxist sense, one is almost tempted to say: as fellow traveler. Nestroy
himself refutes this in one of his songs with the recurring line: "Wenn
Freiheit wird Kommunismus, nein — dann hört's auf ein Vergnügen zu
sein!" (When freedom becomes communism, it ceases to be fun).

aristocrats and commoners and, more recently, between the
rich and the poor. But Nestroy is as critical of the common
people as he is of the rich, the aristocrats, the authorities, fate.
Common people, too, sell their souls for money, with down-to-
earth rationalizations: "I really shouldn't take your money but
one needs money to live, and I live all the time, so I need
money all the time." He sees the common man's weaknesses,
his laziness, his superstition, his adulation of success, his
fickleness. "To get a job would create prosperity, prosperity
might grow into wealth, with wealth come new wishes, wishes
result in dissatisfaction — no, you don't tempt me, I'd rather
remain unemployed." And: "A poor man must eat too. When
he smells food, all other passions disappear. He has no anger,
no emotions, no sadness, no love, no hate, not even a soul. He
has nothing but an appetite."

Nestroy lived at the time when the struggle between absolu-
tism and constitutional freedom was being waged throughout
Europe — a Europe that had been stirred up by the successful
American and French revolutions. But after Napoleon's defeat,
the Holy Alliance among Russia, Prussia, and Austria had re-
sulted in repressive governments for Europe, masterminded
by Prince Metternich, Austria's Minister of Foreign Affairs.
Only for a brief moment in Nestroy's time, in 1848, Europe
stirred again. But when Nestroy joined in manning the bar-
ricades even his contemporaries did not know whether this
was Nestroy the revolutionary or Nestroy the comedian putting
on a parody of a revolutionary. (Just as his contemporaries
never knew whether Nestroy, when taking a curtain call — a
tall, thin man doubling over from the waist and spreading his
long arms — was seriously thanking his fans or caricaturing an
actor taking a bow.) Metternich had to flee to England, and
Nestroy, for a short time, had his chance to spell out, and not
just to hint at, what he thought of censorship. "Censorship is
an admission of the rulers that all they can do is to kick

ignorant slaves around, they can't govern free people," and "Censorship is a pencil turned into a man or a man turned into a pencil, a line personified, drawn through the products of the mind, a crocodile lurking at the banks of the stream of ideas, ready to bite off the heads of the writers."

He used the brief spell of freedom to write some plays dealing with the political ferment of his time, but when they reached the stage the counter-revolution had been successful and the plays were either emasculated or suppressed. Nestroy's enthusiasm for the people's cause was short-lived; he had had hopes both before and during the revolution, but was disappointed by the way the people used their short victory. "The people are a giant in the cradle who wakes up, staggers about, tramples everything down, and in the end collapses, finding himself in a position even more uncomfortable than in the cradle."

Nestroy has been called a skeptic and nihilist, a poet, a prophet, and a philosopher, and he was all of these. In one mood he could call out bitterly, "What has posterity done for me? Nothing! Well, I'll do the same for posterity!" In another mood he speculated about the significance of daydreams: "If they're full of hope, you're young; if they're full of memories you're old." Soberly he lectured, "Principles are tight clothes — they hinder every movement." But philosophical poetry shows through his criticism of man: "Beautiful days are the privilege of the rich but beautiful nights are the monopoly of the happy"; and, similarly: "In a castle in the air even the janitor in the basement has a view into paradise."

Nestroy was maligned, misunderstood, and ignored by his contemporary critics, but his message comes clearly through in the twentieth century: Imperfect man lives in an imperfect world, and improvement is not possible unless he looks at himself critically and unsparingly. This bitter pill of self-examination is best swallowed in a humorous coating. "Seriousness," said Nestroy, "has a solemn side, a sad side, and many grave sides, but it always has a little spot of electricity from which, with the proper friction, the sparks of humor fly."

Methods of Playwriting

When Nestroy came back to Vienna from the provinces in 1831, he continued his established policy of adapting plots and plays from existing sources. He screened German, French, and English plays and novels and took his plots where he found them. This had long been accepted procedure among European playwrights, including Shakespeare and Molière. Europe was still a playwright's paradise; he did not have to invent his plots, he had only to "find" them.

Nestroy raided German (mostly Berlin) farces, French vaudeville plays, English comedies, operettas, operas, and novels, including Charles Dickens' *Martin Chuzzlewit*.[16] In addition, he wrote parodies of works he felt were fake romantic or bombastic, including Richard Wagner's *Tannhäuser* and *Lohengrin*, Giacomo Meyerbeer's *Robert der Teufel*, and plays by Karl von Holtei. In his popular parody of Friedrich Hebbel's *Judith und Holofernes* he poked fun at the sham idolizing of historical and mythological figures, an art which Bernard Shaw later lifted to sophisticated levels.

Nestroy found an ensemble of outstanding comedians in the Vienna Carl Theater and Theater an der Wien. According to an old Viennese saying, a comedian must either be tall and thin, or short and fat, or talented. In Nestroy's repertory theater group he himself was tall and thin, Wenzel Scholz was short and fat, and both were eminently talented. All the plays contain a Nestroy part, a Scholz part, and usually parts written for other members of the cast — for an actor who used

[16] Used in Nestroy's *Die Anverwandten*. Otto Rommel, *Johann Nestroy*, vol. 1 (Vienna: Anton Schroll & Co., 1948)

to play the part of Hanswurst, the comic character in the old
farces, for the great diva, the villain, the dashing young man,
the foolish young thing, the old comedienne, the coquettish
maidservant. It speaks for Nestroy's creative gift that, in
adapting his sources and shaping them into new plays, he
never produced stereotypes but rather new challenges for the
same actors. In the three plays selected for this volume, the
Nestroy parts include a blasé rich man looking for excitement
(*A Man Full of Nothing*), a bitter, basically honest man,
crushed by hostility and prejudice (*Talisman*), and a cynical
scoundrel ready to make his fortune by fair or foul means
(*Love Affairs and Wedding Bells*). When Nestroy adapted
borrowed plots he was usually satisfied with writing juicy
parts for himself and his colleagues and creating amusing
situations, but rarely bothered to change the construction: if
the source play was poorly constructed, so was his own. What
he was looking for was an opportunity to clown. His plays
abound in funny disguises and primitive misunderstandings
that lead to colossal and, by modern standards, often unneces-
sary mixups — people hiding behind curtains, unlikely chance
meetings, and just plain fun, even if it interferes with the plot
and stops the show. In fact, this is sometimes the purpose.

Nestroy was skillful in transplanting foreign settings to
Vienna soil and in pumping blood into the often pale characters of the originals. Under his hands even minor parts became
people as his Vienna audience knew them. Most characters of
Nestroy's plays who look like prototypes of nineteenth-century
Austrians, and some of whom have become part of Austrian
folklore, are "foreigners," naturalized by Nestroy's pen. So
thorough was the transformation that even people who knew
the original play did not recognize the characters when they
saw Nestroy's version on the stage.[17]

The plots may have been borrowed, the characters adapted,

[17] Rommel, *op. cit.* vol. 4

but the dialogue was unadulterated Nestroy, entirely his own property. His plays are sprinkled with witticisms, puns, and homespun philosophy rolled into quips which were drawn, like iron filings to a magnet, into the parts he wrote for himself. His rapid-fire, hair-raising tongue twisters supported the belief, after his death, that only he could have played these parts.

Tradition and Revolution

Nestroy combined literary tradition and innovation. He kept enough of the familiar format of the old Hanswurst comedies to make his audience forget (or pay little attention to) his indictment of the *status quo*. He still used the device of letting his characters talk in asides, to indicate their thoughts. He did not shrink from *deus ex machina* solutions: in his early plays demigods or magicians appeared; later the unexpected denouement came through sudden inheritances, the popping up of a long-lost father, or the discovery of a letter that explained all. Nestroy used verbal "leitmotifs" to identify his characters, a device of many European writers including Dickens ("Barkis is willin'," "I'm confidently expecting something to turn up"), but for comic effect. He also used crudely expressive names to label his characters — a stupid farmer is named Kraut and a sausagemaker, Lard — a technique still retained in comic strips, where a detective is named Dick Tracy. Nestroy also employed the familiar device (surviving in musicals) of characters forgetting about the plot and singing songs.

Here Nestroy really combined the old and the new. He himself was delighted when he had a chance to sing. His voice may no longer have been good enough for grand opera, but it was capable of presenting three or four little ditties an evening. All his plays are "farces with songs" or "parodies with songs" or, in his early days, "fairy plays with songs."

Here again he stands with both feet in the tradition of the Viennese folk comedies, and here again he pioneers. Some of his songs are no more than pleasant excuses for buffoonery. But in most of them — he wrote more than two hundred — the actor steps not only to the footlights but out of the play altogether, and addresses the audience on subjects of general and usually topical interest. The songs are Nestroy's comments on his contemporary world. They are not necessarily concerned with the plot, but always with man, his follies, customs, weaknesses, and anything else that can be got past the censor. Each stanza ends in a punch line that can be passed on with a wink: "Ja, die Männer ham's gut" ("Yes, a man has it made"); "Na, lass' ma an jeden sein' Freud'" ("Let each man be happy, as each man sees fit"); "Das ist wohl nur Chimäre, aber mich unterhalt's" ("This may be all nonsense, but I think it's fun"). The custom of adding stanzas as encores gave Nestroy the opportunity to comment on last-minute events, and netted him fines and jail terms. His songs are the ancestors of the ballads Bertolt Brecht used in his plays and of those ditties that became so popular in the German and Austrian political cabarets during the last years of the Kaiser and between the two world wars, especially during the rise of totalitarianism. These songs abound in innuendo and veiled references, and seem to thrive when freedom of speech is threatened, when people are not allowed to criticize their government openly. In the United States the political *chanson*, by European standards, leads a relatively feeble existence.

The Language

Nestroy's greatness, it has been said,[18] rested on his gift of knowing what needed to be satirized, his wit, and his linguistic artistry. Although the latter kept this Austrian Aristophanes from becoming known outside the reach of his local idiom, he

[18] Battaglia, *op cit.*

was not a dialect writer like Finley Peter Dunne or the authors of such comic strips as the Katzenjammer Kids. He used
language as the carrier for the imagery of his wit; he used
language on all levels, mother tongue in cheek. He parodied
the stilted, lazy elegance of the speech in the Vienna salons;
he satirized the would-be smartness of the *nouveaux riches,*
mocked the officialese of civil servants, and made full use of
the colorful and inventive idiom of the Viennese spoken by
the people in the suburbs. Since most of the Nestroy and
Scholz parts are "common people," the punchiest lines are
spoken in dialect, but even the "lowest" people do not speak
dialect all the time. Nestroy effectively played one kind of
speech against the other. A cobbler who tries to converse with
a nobleman in the highfalutin terms of an aristocrat and, in
the midst of it, drops a real lowdown slang word, or a *parvenu*
who is out to impress a nobleman with a diction he thinks is
aristocratic, provides for more chuckles than would someone
speaking straight dialect.

Nestroy was an educated man, a graduate of Austria's best
high school, and a theater-obsessed dropout from the Univer-
sity of Vienna after two years of law study.[19] In his plays he
draws some of his quips from classical literature or mythology
("Jupiter set an example for all lovers when he disguised himself as a bull to win Europa, and ever since then, bull has
proved effective in winning a girl's heart.")[20] He uses Latin

---

[19] Nestroy went to Austria's best *Gymnasium,* a private school belonging
to the Benedictines, well known for their educational, scholarly, and
literary pursuits. Many of Austria's outstanding citizens went to this
school, including a son of Prince Metternich, many members of the
aristocracy, the poets Friedrich Halm and Eduard von Bauernfeld, and
the painter Moritz Schwind. Battaglia, *op. cit.*

[20] "Für die Lieb' ist keine Verkleidung zu schlecht, wenn sie nur zweck-
mässig ist. Darin hat Jupiter allen Liebhabern ein gutes Beispiel gegeben;
in was für Verkleidungen ist der erschienen, namentlich dazumal, wie er
unserm Weltteil als Ochs entgegenkam." (*Liebesgeschichten und Heiratssachen*)

phrases to poke fun at stuffy bureaucrats or to coin verbal monstrosities (one of his characters who is confident of quick success says: "I feel venividivicious today"). A smattering of English, French, Italian, and Spanish helps him to make bilingual puns. In one scene, an uneducated tailor tries to impress a lady by helping her recover a sharp-toothed little dog she has lost in Italy. He dictates a notice: "Cane perduto. Piccolo pooch with quattro footsies. Denti plenti."[21]

But Nestroy's real tool was, of course, German, the language he truly mastered as a virtuoso. He combined Viennese idiom and High German into similes, metaphors, mixed-up proverbs, and gyrating figures of speech. His word creations may have been primitive or ingenious, but they were never an end in themselves; they always conveyed the message he wanted to get across. "The great of the earth are all stars; that's why they can shine only when everything else is dark." "The words of a thousand imps become important, they impress, because the imps are a thousand, and honest people, who won't believe them, are at most ten."[22] One of the most widely quoted passages comes from a scene in which Nestroy, dressed up as a schoolboy, has to take a test in social studies. To the teacher's question, "What is man?" Nestroy's answer is a display of verbal somersaults which, however, never lose sight of the direction in which they are going. Any attempt to translate such gymnastics must be content with imitation:

Man is a being who occupies the highest stage of creation, who even claims to have been made in the image of God — but God is probably not very flattered. Man is an insect, because he stings, bites, bugs you, gives you the creeps,

[21] *Lumpazivagabundus,* Act II, scene 16: "Hund verloren. Piccolo Viech mit quattro Haxen. Keine Zähne: Zani kani . . . ."
[22] "Was tausend Wichte sagen, bekommt Gewicht, wird wichtig, weil die Wichte tausend sind und die Ehrenmänner, die's nicht glauben, höchstens zehn." (*Der Schützling*)

and is often for the birds. But man is also a fish, because
he gets into deep water and does horrible things in cold
blood. No less is man a reptile, for he's a snake in the
grass. He's a bird, too, because he lives in the clouds, often
makes a living out of thin air, and gets upset when he
cannot fill the bill. And, finally, man is also a mammal,
because he's a sucker.[23]

Nestroy exploited the peculiarities of German, for example
its tendency to form excessively long words. He fired word
rockets that have up to two dozen syllables, and he enjoyed
rattling them off on the stage with the dexterity of a juggler.
Nestroy played with the language like a child who has discovered a new toy. If some of his expressions are clichés today,
it must be remembered that he coined them first. Had he been
writing in English, he probably would have had no compunc-
tion about constructing "progress" as the opposite to "Con-
gress," in forming from "toy" a diminutive "toilet," or from
"infant" a collective "infantry." A second-hand suitor, a dirty
laundry maid, a man with a "rhinocerous" nose may have
popped up — his audience appreciated such burlesques, but it
took two or three generations for the realization that beyond

[23] "Der Mensch ist das Wesen, welches die oberste Stufe in der sichtbaren
Schöpfung einnimmt, welches sich sogar für das Ebenbild Gottes ausgibt,
worüber sich jedoch Gott nicht sehr geschmeichelt fühlen dürfte. Der
Mensch ist ein Säugetier, denn er saugt sehr viel Flüssigkeit in sich, das
Männchen Bier und Wein, das Weibchen Kaffee. Der Mensch ist aber
auch ein Fisch, denn er tut oft Unglaubliches mit kaltem Blut, und hat
auch Schuppen, die ihm zwar plötzlich, aber doch g'wöhnlich zu spät
von den Augen fallen. Der Mensch ist ferner auch ein Wurm, denn er
krümmt sich häufig im Staube und kommt auf diese Art vorwärts. Der
Mensch ist nicht minder ein Amphibium, welches auf dem Lande und
im Wasser lebt, denn mancher, der schon recht im Wasser is, zieht noch
ganz nobel aufs Land hinaus. Der Mensch ist endlich auch ein Federvieh,
denn gar mancher zeigt, wie er a Feder in die Hand nimmt, dass er ein
Vieh ist." (*Die schlimmen Buben in der Schule*)

the punning, catchy songs, and cheap mixups, Nestroy had elevated the lowest form of comedy to the level of literature.

The Selections

In making the three selections for this volume, we had to choose from eighty-three plays. That we will be criticized for their choice seems inevitable. All we can say is that we liked these three plays, thought them amusing and characteristic of Nestroy, and hence suitable for an introduction.

Thus, no attempt is made to defend the omission of any of the other eighty plays, except for the two great favorites, *Lumpazivagabundus* and *Einen Jux will er sich machen.*

Lumpazivagabundus was Nestroy's first hit; it made him famous, and he played in it 259 times. In it he still uses the framework of the world of magic: the king of the good fairies and the patron saint of the vagabonds (the title part) make a bet whether bums will be bums even if they win a fortune in the lottery. The test is made on three unemployed: a cobbler, a tailor, and a carpenter. The first two waste their money on wine, women, and song, but the carpenter becomes a thrifty family man, saved by true love. The play has three magnificent parts, plenty of antics, and Nestroy's most famous song. The cobbler, an amateur astrologer, is certain that a comet will soon destroy the earth, and sings, almost yodels, that catch line: "Die Welt steht auf kein' Fall mehr lang," — "The world will for sure not last long." As so often, Nestroy's line speaks directly to our industrial atomic era and permits timely adaptations. Still, *Lumpazivagabundus* is not included here because its roots are more Viennese and less universal than most of Nestroy's other works and because it is a badly constructed play, despite its popularity.[24]

[24] Weigel, *op. cit.* (above, n. 3.)

Einen Jux will er sich machen was omitted because it has been pre-empted by Thornton Wilder's adaptation. Although *The Matchmaker* is mostly Wilder, there is enough Nestroy in it to duplicate values.

The three plays selected were written during Nestroy's peak production period, 1840-1844, in which he wrote fifteen plays. *A Man Full of Nothing* has always been one of the great Nestroy favorites. In it Nestroy satirizes Byronism, and "his fight against sentimentalism is more effective than that of his famous contemporary Heinrich Heine," as the Vienna playwright and critic Egon Friedell commented.[25] In this play Nestroy exposes what in his time was an affectation of the few, but has since become one of the major problems of our time: man's feeling of inner emptiness and of the meaninglessness of his life. Nestroy diagnoses nineteenth-century *Weltschmerz*, the sentimental pessimism among poets, writers, and upper-class idlers, as boredom; his hero is a rich man who does not know what to do with himself and who finds that he needs the thrill of crime and police chase to stimulate his will to live. In the second half of the twentieth century a disintegration of values, fear of atomic war, and a fatalism caused by man's feeling of helplessness in the face of powerful forces have spread this disease of an inner void to juvenile gangs, divorce courts, and society pages. Psychotherapists have coined a name for it: "existential frustration." It may be coincidence or inspiration, but Nestroy's overused cure-all, love, turns out to be that of modern psychologists, also. For example, both Erich Fromm and Viktor Frankl prescribe it as a cure for this disease of inner emptiness.

A Man Full of Nothing is one of Nestroy's most winsome comedies, full of droll dialogue and buffoonery; it presents a string of memorable characters, including popular Nestroy and

[25] Egon Friedell, *op. cit.*

Scholz parts and one of his most touching women's roles (he shies away from anything mushy or syrupy). The supporting parts are drawn with unusual care.

The Talisman, an immediate success, remained forgotten for many years. It was recently revived, however, both in print and on the German-speaking stage when, as with so many of Nestroy's works, the appeal shifted from the play's surface to its depth. A certain leniency is required of modern audiences, particularly Americans, in accepting a nineteenth-century Austrian folk prejudice that red-haired people are both dishonest and firebugs. In our world, where redheads get wolf calls, it is difficult to realize that they were once victims of discrimination, particularly in the isolated Alpine villages of Austria, where persons with red hair were rare and therefore suspect because they were "different." *The Talisman* was popular in Nestroy's time because it gave the main character an opportunity to disguise himself, in the course of the play, with the help of a number of different-colored wigs, and to get into numerous jams. Today, the appeal lies more in Nestroy's unmasking of man's discriminatory practices and superstitions. The play contains one of the strongest Nestroy parts (Titus), a female lead of great tenderness (Salome), and a powerful ending.

Love Affairs and Wedding Bells was originally a mild success. It is included in this volume because it provides an example of a typical light Nestroy farce with three couples being led through a series of well-constructed mixups and "plain fun" situations. It presents one of Nestroy's favorite themes: the conflict between tradition-ridden aristocrats of the dying feudal era and the vulgar, pseudo-elegant, newly rich capitalists. It also includes a prototype of Nestroy's popular characters: the nimble-witted, scheming cynic without conscience or heart, who gets himself into trouble by sheer bravado, and out again by mental somersaults.

The Translation

In attempting to recreate Nestroy's imagery of words, his
spatter of puns, his circus act of straddling the twin horses of
Viennese slang and High German, we aimed at preserving his
flavor rather than his words. Direct translation was used where
feasible, approaches and analogies where it was not.

Those familiar with Nestroy will note with alarum or charity
that we have slightly (but always fondly) tampered with his
plays. The outdated was dropped, the asides reduced, some
gaps filled. Occasionally, where the sparkle of Nestroy's for-
mulations dimmed in translation, a linguistic bolt of lightning
was borrowed from other Nestroy plays or, more forward still,
words were supplied in terms Nestroy might conceivably have
used had he enjoyed the resources of the English language.
Such liberties, considered sacrilegious with other classics, are
part of a tradition going back to Nestroy himself. Partly because of censorship, partly because of his fondness for adlib-
bing, Nestroy often changed his own dialogue as he played
his part. Several versions of the same scenes exist in various
notebooks and actors' work copies. When Karl Kraus revived
Nestroy in 1912, he reworked some of the comedies, reducing
the obsolete and stressing what had become significant since
the playwright's death; and that practice has become standard
procedure in modern Nestroy productions. In some instances
his plays are extensively adapted and rewritten. Hans Weigel,
reviewing a 1950 production of *Lumpazivagabundus* in Vienna, wrote: "The majority of the funny ideas are not the
author's but have become tradition in the course of subsequent
stage presentations; the ending of the second act and the ending of the play are freshly invented by every stage director."[26]

[26] Hans Weigel, *Tausend und eine Premiere* (Vienna: Wollzeilen Verlag,
1961)

The tampering is most noticeable in the songs. As in Nestroy's time and in all contemporary productions of his plays, some stanzas are added, others omitted; some choruses were borrowed from other Nestroy plays. The songs were Nestroy's way of social criticism, and his encores, often written for a particular production, were his up-to-date comments on the foibles of fellow citizens. We trust we have not done violence to Nestroy's spirit by using his songs to hold up a mirror not only to nineteenth-century Austrians but also to twentieth-century Americans.

What remains to be said is a word of caution. The flattering adjectives used in this introduction refer, of course, to the original Nestroy. May there be no disappointment, after such a glowing announcement, if the translation does not come up to expectations. "Translating from one language to another," as a much-quoted passage from Cervantes says, "is like gazing at a Flemish tapestry with the wrong side out." The reasons why translators have not been able to convey the savage irony imbedded in the shape of Nestroy's language, are as valid today as they have been for the past hundred years. In making our attempt, we are aware that half its delight becomes lost in translation; but we also feel that Nestroy's genius is strong enough to shine through the violations we have felt obliged to commit against him.

M. K. and J. F.

A Man
Full of Nothing

(DER ZERRISSENE)

A Farce with Songs, in Three Acts

Johann Nestroy and his co-star Wenzel Scholz as Lips and Redhot in Act Three of *A Man Full of Nothing* (*Der Zerrissene*). The play was first performed on April 9, 1844, and during the next fifteen years Nestroy played the title role 107 times. Etching from the first edition of the play, 1845.

Today, *A Man Full of Nothing* is still a favorite on the Austrian stage. Sophisticated audiences enjoy Nestroy's mocking of what has become, a hundred years later, the "existential meaninglessness" of life that prompts people to seek thrills in dares. The scene shows Lips announcing to his friends that he is going to marry the first woman who crosses his path. From a recent production at the Tiroler Landestheater, Innsbruck, Austria.

CHARACTERS

Herr von Lips
Boot ⎫
Heel ⎬ his friends
Polish ⎭
Madame Veil
Redhot, a blacksmith
Peter Kraut, leaseholder on one of Lips's farms
Kathy, his niece
Justice of the Will
Anton ⎫
Joseph ⎬ servants of Lips
Christian ⎭
Farmhands of Kraut

Time and place: Mid-nineteenth-century Austria

ACT ONE

(*The house of Herr von Lips, an elegant country house near Vienna. Doors left and right; in the center a glass door leading onto a balcony, with a view of a picturesque gorge. Left and right tables and chairs. Behind the center door a couch.*)

Scene 1

ANTON (*to Christian and Joseph each of whom carries three champagne bottles*): Bring them right in, they won't be the last. Once these people start drinking . . .

JOSEPH: Yes, he wines and dines his guests, our chief.

CHRISTIAN: Not just his guests. He fills himself pretty well, too.

JOSEPH: I don't get it. How can a man with all that good wine in his cellar have such a vinegar face?

ANTON: You wouldn't understand. He's trying to drown his troubles in wishful drinking. Inside, he's all broken up, and the champagne runs right through the cracks, instead of going to his head. But that's none of your business; get going and serve!

CHRISTIAN (*leaving with Joseph*): Broken up inside — with all that money?

JOSEPH: Ha, he can afford to be "broken up" — I'm just plain broke.

(*Exits right with Christian.*)

33

Scene 2

ANTON (*looking toward the balcony*):   When the whole ca-
boodle comes out here and Herr von Lips sees that the railing on the balcony hasn't been fixed yet, I'll catch it again.

(*Redhot enters carrying part of a heavy iron balcony railing; helper who carries another part enters
also, places it on the balcony, and leaves.*)

REDHOT: Whew! This railing must weigh a ton!
ANTON: Well, it's about time. I thought you had forgotten
all about us, Redhot.
REDHOT: It takes an hour to get here from my place empty-
handed. With a load like this, and if you have to stop for
a nip here and there, half a day is gone before you know it.
ANTON: Yes, those nips have boggled me, too.
REDHOT: Won't take a minute now, though. (*Steps to the
balcony and puts the railing in place.*)
ANTON: Makes you shiver, doesn't it, to look down into that
water from the balcony?
REDHOT: I'll say. Water in any form gives me the shivers.
ANTON: If this was my house I'd have walled up the window
that used to be here. But no, the chief has to put in a French
door and build a balcony — and all for a view! Nuts, I say.
REDHOT: Well, here we go! (*Starts whacking at the railing.*)
ANTON: Whoa! Keep quiet. There's a banquet going on in
the next room.
REDHOT: Well, you can't fasten a railing with spit and a
prayer.
ANTON: I don't care. No banging now.
REDHOT: Suits me. I'll leave it stand here, and come back
later. (*He puts his hammer away. Toasts are heard from the*

banquet room: *"Three cheers for Lips!"*) Quite a party they're having. Your chief must be a gay dog!

ANTON: His guests are the gay dogs, not him. I'll see if they need more champagne.

(*Exits right.*)

Scene 3

REDHOT (*alone*): These rich people live some life! They drink, eat, sleep, and make merry all day. Too bad: I'd have had a great talent for being rich, if only one of those millionnaires would have given me lessons. If he'd made me an apprentice and then turned the business over to me — I think I might have made a go of it!

KATHY (*entering center left*): They said that's where I'd find Herr von Lips. (*Sees Redhot.*) Why, look who's here? Redhot, the locksmith!

REDHOT (*studying Kathy and trying to place her*): Wait till I find the key to my memory.

KATHY: It's me — Kathy Kraut!

REDHOT: Well, so it is! How's Pete Kraut, my old pal?

KATHY: Angry at you, that's what he is, because you haven't come to the farm for a year and a half. And he's right, too. A fine friend you are! The farm is only a few hours from the city.

REDHOT: I'm not living in the city now. But what are you doing here? Did Kraut send you to bring the rent?

KATHY: Do I always have to be running errands for Uncle Kraut? Can't I have some business of my own?

REDHOT: Why, of course, your business is none of my business.

KATHY: You were right about one thing: I came to make a payment. You know that Herr von Lips is my godfather?

REDHOT: You owe him money for that?

KATHY: My mother was a maid with old Herr von Lips, before she set up as a seamstress. When the young Herr von Lips got all that money and bought up Uncle Kraut's farm and all those others, we never dared come near him, he was so rich. But three years ago when we were so desperate . . . Sewing don't pay much . . .

REDHOT: Same as a milliner's work. I know all about it.

KATHY: How would a blacksmith know about hat-making?

REDHOT (*sighing*):   Oh, I was a milliner, too!

KATHY: You don't mean it!

REDHOT: Yes, I do. In the course of events all will become clear.

KATHY: Go on! Tell me!

REDHOT: Let's hear your story first.

KATHY: It's almost finished. When we reached the end of our rope, and mother was sick, I took heart and went to my godfather for a loan of a hundred thalers. He handed it to me right away and just laughed when I talked about paying it back. But I promised Mother before she died not to forget our debt. So I went to work for Uncle Kraut, and I worked and I saved, and I saved and I worked, and now after three years of scraping and scrimping I have the money, and I've come here to pay it.

REDHOT: Paying debts — that's a luxury I can't afford any more.

KATHY: How can you talk like that — a master blacksmith and locksmith in good standing!

REDHOT: Ha, master! For the past five months I've been an apprentice again, and I'm looking back on my mastership, walleyed, like a crab.

KATHY (*sympathetically*):   What happened?

REDHOT: In the course of events all will become clear. Two years ago I fell in love with a laundress — a pure, clean soul. She wanted to be a milliner, so I got an old hatmaker to take her on as an apprentice. I tell you, my poppet was a natural — soon she made better hats than the boss. Then the old milliner died — this was our chance. We decided to tie the knot, so I agreed to buy the store for my intended. I paid half the 4,000 thalers down, and we fixed the day for the wedding. Then . . . (*Sighs.*)

KATHY: Don't tell me *she* died, too.

REDHOT (*sadly*): In the course of events all will become clear. The date was set, the wedding dress bought, my Sunday suit altered for the occasion . . . (*Sobs*) the veil ironed, the guests invited — cost me two thalers per person — (*Chokes up*) plus the drinks . . .

KATHY: Come on, pull yourself together.

REDHOT: The day before the wedding I went to her place. She wasn't there.

KATHY: What happened?

REDHOT: In the course of events — no, it never did become clear. She never came home again. I've looked for her high and low, told the police, tried to find relatives — nothing helped. Her disappearance rocked my whole life — I've had rocks in my head ever since.

KATHY: Oh, you'll get over it!

REDHOT: Never. One thing led to another: here I was, the owner of a milliner's shop, although I still owed 2,000 thalers. So I closed my blacksmith shop and started to make hats.

KATHY: What an idea!

REDHOT: Oh, the idea wasn't so bad but people didn't give me a chance. They came and tried on hats — not to buy them but just for laughs. The old customers said I had no taste because I had done all the hats in coal black and fiery red. They called them hatrocities. Very funny. After four months I was bankrupt, and to get away from my creditors

I went to the country and hired myself out as a blacksmith's apprentice. That's the full course of events as they
became clear. O Mathilda!

KATHY: Oh, forget her, the ungrateful witch!

REDHOT: How can you say that? She was kidnapped, she's
kept captive, and she has no other thought than to fly back
into my arms.

KATHY: Gracious me, you think so?

REDHOT: I do, I do. If only I could get hold of those kid-
nappers! I tell you, Kathy . . . (*Takes her hand.*) . . . I'd clamp
down on them . . . (*Twists Kathy's hand.*) . . . turn the
screws on them . . .

KATHY: Ouch, go easy . . . I'm not a kidnapper.

REDHOT: Oh, I'm sorry, but I tell you if a blacksmith gets
fired up . . .

Scene 4

ANTON (*from the banquet room*): Better move on, you two.
Herr von Lips is about to come out with his guests.

KATHY: Oh, good . . . then I can talk to him.

ANTON: No, you can't. Not now.

KATHY: I'll wait outside then.

ANTON: Take a walk in the garden.

REDHOT: And I'll fix the railing later.

ANTON: Righto.

REDHOT: Come, Kathy. Mathilda is lost . . . but I'll find him,
that Mathilda-snatcher. (*Grimly*) And when I do, I'll go
at him hammer and tongs! (*Takes her arm.*)

KATHY: Ouch! Don't try it out on me!

REDHOT: I'm sorry — there are moments when the blacksmith in me forges to the front, and there's not a trace of the
milliner left in my head. (*Exits with Kathy.*)

ANTON (*looking toward the banquet room*): Here comes
the chief — and with a face as long as the Friday before
payday!

(*Exits.*)

Scene 5

LIPS (*entering from center right*):

SONG

I'm full of the best kind of food and of likker,
My clothes and my shoes every season get slicker,
And yet I'm in shreds and I'm falling apart —
I am just a man full of nothing at heart.
My inside is empty, my spirit a hole,
And there isn't a shop where they patch up a soul.
But if someone should ask me why all this should be,
I just couldn't say what's the matter with me:
   It's a terrible thing when you find
   That you don't even know your own mind.

At times for a trip round the world I am itchin',
At times it's too far from my bed to my kitchen.
Sometimes I invite a few dozens of guests,
As soon as they come, I could kick out the pests.
One day I believe I like life pretty well,
The next day I'd just as soon go straight to hell.
I sometimes like women, a whole harem for fun,
Then sometimes, again, I can't stand even one.
   It's a terrible thing when you find
   That you don't even know your own mind.

Encore

Why a man is neurotic, his inside a void,
Was discovered years later in Vienna by Freud.
What Nestroy suspected, the great doctor proved:
Your inside is torn 'cause your mother once goofed.
By offering a bottle instead of a nipple
She nipped in the bud, ah, your pleasure principle.
She smashed you to bits in a subconscious wreckup,
So *you* need a checkup each week from the neck up.
　It's a terrible thing when you find
　That you don't even know your own mind.

Poverty is without doubt the worst calamity: If someone offered me ten million thalers to be poor — I wouldn't take them. On the other hand, what's so good about being rich? The fuller your wallet the emptier is your life. If a brat yells for no good reason, you show him the bare facts of life by licking the pants off him. But for a kid of my age fate would have to do the licking. Not a chance. If you're rich, you're in luck and there's nothing to lick: my money is safely salted away, my valuables insured, and only a giant snail could carry away my houses. And death can't rob me of a dear relative because I don't have any. I'm the only one in my family who could die, and I'm not going to kill myself mourning for me. I couldn't even get a kick out of a mule. Just now I'm giving a feast, but how can I kill time until the next? Love? Gambling? Gambling is no fun for the rich — losing doesn't hurt and winning doesn't matter. And love? That's a laugh. Even love is no adventure for the rich, money clears all obstacles. Can I secretly steal into a girl's room? Mama is there to let me in. Am I thrown down the stairs by an angry father? No, he has the servants respectfully lead me up, light in hand. Are dogs sicked on me? Is water poured on my head? No, Papa and Mama insist that I come again. And the husbands? Do they hit me? For a loan, maybe. Oh, for an old-fashioned, hot-blooded husband who would want to shoot me — I'd get a bang out of that! No, no, I can give as many banquets as I want, at the banquet of life I only get stale crumbs, and even these I can keep down only with the help of my friends. That's one thing a rich man can't complain about — a lack of friends! How faithfully they share my table! How loyally they join me in every binge! They cling to me for dear life. I really am an enviable fellow — trouble is, I don't envy myself!

Scene 6

BOOT (*entering with Heel and Polish, to Lips*): I say, friend, what's the matter? You keep getting quieter, just when we're all getting louder. Your face darkens just when our faces light up . . .

POLISH (*swaying*): Yes . . . we're all lit up, I'd say.

BOOT: The guests are upset because you disappeared and they can't see you . . .

LIPS: That's all right. Before, they saw two of me, so that evens the score.

POLISH: If you're happy we all have a feast. If you're sad we glumly gulp down your food. We are with you in any case.

BOOT AND HEEL: You can always count on us.

LIPS: I surely picked winners, with the three of you. You're friends I can depend on — always around when I throw a party.

BOOT: Come on, have another glass of champagne.

LIPS: What's the use? If I were twenty, maybe . . . but now . . .

POLISH: For me, there's no better time than now.

LIPS: Of course — if a chap is as young as you are.

POLISH: That's right — I'm only fifty-four.

LIPS: But I'm already thirty-eight. It makes no difference what it says on your birth certificate. It's the dreams that tell you how old you are — your daydreams. If they're full of hope, you're young; if they're full of memories, you're old. I have no hopes and I remember plenty, so I'm an old fossil. Life has passed me by — fate, I'll sue you for damages! My life's worthless.

POLISH: No man is completely worthless; he can always serve as a horrible example. Lips, you need a change.

LIPS: Easily said. How?

POLISH: Take a trip. We'll go with you.

LIPS: Just to see that anywhere else life is as dull as it is here?

BOOT: Not at all. He means the beauty of nature — mountains, volcanoes, waterfalls . . .

LIPS: Name me a country where I can see something new . . . where a waterfall makes a different splash, a forest brook a different murmur, a spring a different gurgle . . . . Show me a volcano that spits snow, an icicle that can burn, grass that's pink. No, friend, nature, too, suffers from an unbearable monotony.

POLISH (*to Heel*):   Why don't you give him some advice, you sham Britisher, you?

HEEL: I say horses, nothing but horses. Keep a racing stable, hire jockeys, go to the races. It'll make a new man of you.

LIPS: No, I'll always be Lips, that's the trouble.

POLISH: Then do something foolish.

HEEL: Jolly good idea!

LIPS: What, for instance?

BOOT: Friend, I've got it! One thing is still new to you: matrimony!

LIPS: Yes, that's one thing that I've stayed away from — I've never made the same mistake once.

BOOT: It all depends on whom you choose. You have to make an original choice.

LIPS: How can I? If I choose sensibly . . . that's been done, though not very often. If I choose stupidly, millions have done it. However . . . if . . . why, wait a minute —

BOOT AND HEEL: Yes?

LIPS: An original choice . . . let me see . . . that's it! I'll choose without a choice.

BOOT: How's that?

LIPS (*with sudden firm decision*): Yes! I'm going to marry the first woman that crosses my path!

BOOT: You're crazy.

POLISH (*simultaneously*): That's nonsense.

LIPS: Angel or hag, young or old, a peach or a lemon — I'll marry her!

HEEL: By Jove, that's most sporting!

BOOT: But what if . . .

LIPS: No ifs or buts. The first woman that comes along. I tell you, friends, I already feel the thrill of this decision, the tension, the curiosity: Who will be the first?

Scene 7

ANTON (*entering from center left*): A Madame Veil wishes to pay her respects.

LIPS: Fate, you're not wasting any time!

ANTON: She says she hasn't had the honor before.

BOOT: Who is she?

ANTON: She has a summer cottage out here.

LIPS: Never mind. Show her in.

ANTON: Yes, Sir. (*Walks toward the door.*)

LIPS (*calling after him*):   Hold it. *Madame* Veil, you said . . .
Be sure and ask her if she's a widow.

ANTON: I will, Sir.

LIPS: And don't let her in unless she is.

ANTON: I won't, Sir.

(*Exits.*)

Scene 8

LIPS (*all worked up*):   Now what do you say, friends?

BOOT: Destiny is in the making.

LIPS (*looking out into the garden*): If she's a widow she'll
come. And if she comes she's a widow.

BOOT: Profound!

LIPS: Now run along, all of you, and leave me alone with
the woman of my choice.

BOOT: For heaven's sake, you don't really mean it, do you?

LIPS: Absolutely . . . I'm going to marry the great unknown!

HEEL: Well, I'll be dashed!

BOOT (*leaving with Heel and Polish*):   Now he's going to
make his original choice. Me and my big mouth!

(*All three leave.*)

LIPS (*alone*):   This is the greatest fascination of my life. For
years I've felt like a prisoner in his death cell — and why
not? Isn't life just a death sentence, pronounced at birth
and stayed for a while? Can a fellow do anything better
than order a choice last meal? And the choicest delicacy,
they say, is love. We'll see . . .

Scene 9

ANTON (*entering from center left, with Madame Veil*):   The
widowed Madame Veil. (*Exits.*)

LIPS: It's a pleasure indeed.

VEIL (*dressed elegantly but loudly*): Please forgive me, Herr von Lips . . .

LIPS: What can I do for you, Madame?

VEIL: I'm organizing a ball, a light affair . . .

LIPS: All light shows better on a dark background. No doubt, your ball is for charity?

VEIL: One might say so, yes, inasmuch as it is charitable to give people pleasure.

LIPS: I see . . . and inasmuch as the proceeds from the ball have a charitable effect upon the treasury of the organizer.

VEIL: And inasmuch as the effect upon the organizer's creditors is most charitable.

LIPS: In brief, the ball is organized in the best interests of your creditors. Now if you get the best of your guests, everything will turn out for the best, right?

VEIL: Herr von Lips, you make merry with a widow who has been forced by circumstances . . .

LIPS: You're right, I apologize.

VEIL (*sighing*): I should never have taken that Veil!

LIPS: I beg your pardon?

VEIL: I took him, but heaven took him from me again.

LIPS: I see — Veil was the name of your late husband?

VEIL: Right.

LIPS: And he left you without means?

VEIL: None, except a little summer cottage. I'm getting some income by renting out rooms to summer guests. But now my creditors want to take it from me.

LIPS: Yes, you can insure your home against fire, but insurance against the most common disaster, the creditors, has not yet been invented.

VEIL: In my desperation I decided to organize that ball, to save the house in which my husband died.

LIPS: I understand — a temple of sweet memories.

VEIL: On the contrary — my priceless memory is that I got rid of him in that house.

LIPS: You're being very sensible — a widow who makes a cult of her former husband doesn't deserve to have him departed.

VEIL: When he died, I decided that it would be foolish to attach my heart to such a transitory creature. My husband — God bless him — never made an honest thaler.

LIPS: And how did he make his dishonest thalers?

VEIL: He operated a laundry.

LIPS: That's a business where you can really clean up.

VEIL: Not he, though. He did me dirt. He married me under false pretenses. I was a laundress myself, and he simply wanted some free help. He came to see me in a horse-drawn carriage. He seemed to have money to burn — the surest way to set the heart of an innocent girl on fire. But the carriage was borrowed, the money embezzled . . .

LIPS: Let's go back to your ball.

VEIL: Oh yes, I have the honor of offering you this ticket . . .

LIPS (*reading*): Price — five thalers . . .

VEIL: The printer failed to add: "No limit to the purchaser's generosity."

LIPS: I don't seem to have small change. Would this hundred-thaler bill be acceptable?

VEIL: Herr von Lips . . . your generosity . . . my warmest thanks . . . (*Hastily*) I'd better not take more of your precious time . . . (*Exits.*)

LIPS (*alone*): Wow, is she in a hurry! She must have an aversion to making change. (*Remembering*) Oh my, I forgot all about her being my bride! (*Runs to the door and calls after her.*) Madame . . . if you don't mind . . . just a moment . . .

VEIL (*returning*): You called? You *do* want change?

LIPS: No, no. That wasn't it.

VEIL: Another ticket maybe?

LIPS: No, thanks. For a bachelor one ticket will do, and even if the bachelor marries the organizer of the ball he only needs one ticket, for the organizer needs no ticket to her own ball.

VEIL: I don't understand.

LIPS: I called you back for just a moment, because I want to join you forever.

VEIL: Five thalers for the ticket, ninety-five thalers for the joke . . . fair enough.

LIPS: But it's no joke — and that's the joke about it.

VEIL: I don't believe my ears.

LIPS: Well — I aim to get married, and it so happens that I'm aiming at you. Isn't that better than aiming a gun at myself?

VEIL: Oh, no!!

LIPS: I'm a man full of nothing, my inside's full of holes . . . like the nightshirt of a tramp. The other night it didn't seem worth patching.

VEIL: You tried to run away from it all?

LIPS: I know there are many who call suicide a coward's way out. Let them try it . . . *then* let them talk. I was all set, but when I drew up my will in favor of some friends, all the fun went out of my suicide. I've postponed the idea, not discarded it. That's the good thing about suicide — you can take your time: eternity is still long enough.

VEIL: So you want to get married instead of shooting yourself? How do you know that you're not going to change your mind about this shotgun wedding, too, and regret it later?

LIPS: That's what happens in marriage, anyway: The whole institution has been set up to trap people . . . so regret won't do them any good. But, come now, Madame, I have been footloose and fiancée-free long enough . . . Your decision . . .

VEIL: I don't know . . . am I dreaming . . . or . . . ?

LIPS: Start play-acting. Pretend that your decision depends not on my position but on my engaging personality.

VEIL: You call it play-acting when a woman hesitates before making the most important decision of her life?

LIPS: Good, good, you're play-acting already. And I deserve it, too. A rich man is easily blinded: he forgets that his brilliance comes from his gold, and he thinks that it is his charm that glitters. He stands knee-deep in his millions, sees nothing but millions in front and in back, and therefore needs no foresight and no hindsight, and hardly any judgment. When I come from a party, do you think I go to my stocks and bonds and thank them for my conquests? Do I kneel down before my cashbox and give credit to my credit? Do I acknowledge that a woman's interest is in my interests? That it is my legal tender to which she responds? No, I plunk myself before the mirror and crow, "I'm the cream of the crop!" So, you see, it serves us successful businessmen right if women give us the business. Go ahead, then, tell me your answer!

VEIL: But, Herr von Lips, give me a few moments to reflect. After all, marriage is an important institution . . .

LIPS: And you are not sure whether you are ready for an institution — I understand perfectly. No question of saying No, but to say Yes, you feel it proper to drag your feet a little. All right, that's fine with me.

Scene 10

KATHY (*from center left*):   Ah, my godfather!

LIPS: What is it, Miss?

KATHY: Don't you recognize me? I'm Kathy, your godchild.

LIPS: Oh yes, it's you. My, you have grown since I saw you last!

KATHY: That was three years ago when you were good enough to lend us . . .

LIPS: Yes, yes, but right now, you see . . . (*Motions her to go away.*)

VEIL: Run along, dearie, you can see Herr von Lips is extremely busy.

KATHY: I just came to pay back our debt.

LIPS: Later, later. I'm in conference now. (*To Veil*) All right, Madame, I'll give you time to think but no more than fifteen minutes.

VEIL: How much can one think in fifteen minutes? Actually, what is there much to think about? You see through all pretense anyway . . . Right now I could . . .

LIPS: I know, you could say Yes right now, but I've come to like the idea of breathlessly waiting for your decision. I'm going to sit here in anxious anticipation — it's a great excitement for me. See, that's how a man fools himself. It's no easy trick. To fool others, all you need is a bunch of addlepates who are stupider than you are; but to fool yourself, you have to outsmart yourself. Well then, fifteen minutes dearly beloved, I shall count the seconds! Let me get into the mood . . . my blood pressure rises, my heart flutters, my stomach is a swarm of butterflies . . . it's a matter of life and death!

(*Exits.*)

Scene 11

VEIL (*to herself*): I have him hooked — if only he doesn't get away! A crazy millionaire is a slippery fish until after he's landed.

KATHY (*to herself*): I'll wait until he comes back. I don't want to take the money back home.

VEIL (*condescendingly to Kathy*): So Herr von Lips is your godfather?

KATHY (*shyly*): Yes, Ma'am.

VEIL: You're bringing him money you owe him? Without being asked?

KATHY: Of course. What one owes one must pay.

VEIL (*to herself*): In this house, the strangest things happen.

KATHY (*picking up courage*): You're so kind to me . . . would you mind if I ask a question . . . it's probably a silly question . . . but I got the notion that my godfather is thinking of getting married.

VEIL: He does have some such plans, yes.

KATHY: He does? And . . . who is the lucky bride if I may ask?

VEIL (*proudly and curtly*): I am.

KATHY (*hiding her emotions*): You? Oh, then he must love you very much. He's such a fine man . . . and he has everything but a loving wife. Oh, you will make him happy.

VEIL (*stiffly*): Are you trying to give me advice on how to make a man happy?

KATHY: Oh, no, no. Please forgive me if I've said the wrong thing.

Scene 12

BOOT (*entering from left*): Well, what happened? (*Looking for Lips*) He isn't here.

VEIL: Whom are you looking for?

BOOT: Pop my buttons! You?

VEIL (*pleasantly surprised*): Ah, this really *is* a surprise. What are you doing here?

Boot: That's what I wanted to ask you, charming and sud-
denly-vanished Mathilda.

Kathy (*to herself*): Mathilda?

Veil: I've had all sorts of strange adventures this past year
and a half; and the latest is that, about five minutes ago, I
became Herr von Lips' bride.

Boot; Why, this is hilarious!

Veil: Imagine catching a goldfish, at a time when it is hard
to land even a toad!

Kathy (*to herself*): What a nasty woman!

Veil: It may be a good idea, Papa Boot . . .

Boot: Charming! "Papa Boot!" That's what delightful Mathilda Fink always used to call me.

Veil: It will be better not to talk about the old times around
here.

Boot: I understand. We never saw each other before. But
you'll find more former admirers of yours around here.
Come into the garden, you'll be surprised.

Veil: But I must be back in ten minutes.

Boot: Of course. Let's go.

Veil: A millionaire who counts the seconds must not be kept
waiting a minute.

(*Exits with Boot.*)

Scene 13

(*During this scene, the background slowly darkens.*)

Kathy (*alone*): I don't know much about marriage but I'll
never believe that such a woman can make a man happy.

Redhot (*rushing in from the left*): Kathy! Kathy! I've seen
something! No one can tell me different!

Kathy: Who wants to tell you different? And what have
you seen?

REDHOT: I've seen something from afar that's very close to my heart . . .

KATHY: You're all in a sweat!

REDHOT: Crack my kidneys — who wouldn't be? I fought and spit and scratched but that stupid Anton took my hammer away.

KATHY: That wasn't stupid at all. Why are you so upset?

REDHOT: I saw a woman here.

KATHY: She left just a moment ago.

REDHOT: Now I'll make your eyes pop. From the distance, the one who left was clearly my one and only.

KATHY: Don't be foolish. That was the bride of Herr von Lips.

REDHOT: I don't believe it.

KATHY: Herr Boot called her Mathilda Fink.

REDHOT (*shouting*): Mathilda Fink?! Fink!? Mathilda!? That's the one!

KATHY: The who?

REDHOT: My kidnapped sweetkins! Here she's been held captive, my light-o'-love! Here she has resisted all the wiles of the kidnapper!

KATHY: This lady here was very friendly with Herr von Lips.

REDHOT: Just to soften up the kidnapper, obviously. Oh, Mathilda to what trickery must you resort! But wait, I'll pry you loose! (*Runs toward the center right.*)

KATHY (*trying to hold him*): What do you want, Master Redhot?

REDHOT: I want his life, nothing less than his crooked life. Where can I get a weapon? I'd give my right arm for a jack knife! My fortune for a pinch of arsenic! A kingdom for a second-hand guillotine!

KATHY: You're terrible!

REDHOT: Yes, terribly stupid to worry about a weapon. These

fists are a locksmith's proper keys to unlock the gates of eternity for the kidnapper!

KATHY: What? No, I won't let you harm Herr von Lips.

REDHOT (*with increasing fury*): Where is he? Speak!

KATHY (*cowed*): In the garden.

REDHOT (*overwhelmed by rage*): Ha! I'll go and congratulate him on his wedding. (*Accompanying each word with a kick, thrust, and blow*) Happiness! Joy! Health! Long life . . . anything his heart desires! Wait, you bride snatcher!

(*Exits.*)

Scene 14

KATHY: Oh heavens, what have I done? I've told on my godfather . . .

BOOT (*with Veil, Heel, and Polish, from the left*): Come in, charming Mathilda, the evening air is getting fresh.

HEEL (*putting his arm around her waist*): And that may give us ideas, too.

POLISH: We take good care of our friend's bride.

VEIL (*freeing herself*): You're too kind, gentlemen.

KATHY (*has run first to the middle door left, then to the right, calling through the closed door*): Herr von Lips! Herr von Lips!

BOOT: What's the matter with that person? Why the commotion?

KATHY: I've got to tell my godfather . . .

BOOT: Impossible. Not now.

VEIL: Go on, child, another time.

KATHY: But, Madame, I must see him . . .

VEIL (*impatiently and harshly*): Another time, I said. And I mean it! (*Points to the door, center left.*)

BOOT (*to Veil*): Pay no attention to her.

KATHY (*frightened, to herself, while withdrawing to the door*): I have to find a servant . . . to warn Herr von Lips.

(*Exits.*)

Scene 15

BOOT: Soon we'll drink to the new lady of the house.

VEIL: Gentlemen, I'm flattered. I'll not forget you — you will find that this house will have a hospitable mistress.

POLISH: Mistress — that's the word.

VEIL: We'll form a small but intimate circle.

POLISH: A circle, a triangle . . . we're not particular about geometry.

VEIL: Don't be naughty. I go along with a little merrymaking, but I have a clean mind.

POLISH: No wonder, you change it often enough.

BOOT: But now we musn't leave friend Lips in suspense any longer.

VEIL: The fifteen minutes must be over . . .

(*Two servants enter with lighted candelabra.*)

BOOT (*to Veil*): Permit me to be the one to bring him the glad tidings. (*Opens door, right. Lips lies asleep on a couch.*) He's asleep!

HEEL AND POLISH (*surprised*): Asleep?

VEIL (*unable to suppress her anger*): Asleep! The nerve!

BOOT: Obviously, the emotional strain and the approaching dusk have brought on a slight slumber. (*Lips snores.*)

VEIL: It seems to be more a slight than a slumber.

POLISH: He is sleeping like a top . . . and humming like one, too.

BOOT (*to servants*): Put the lights on the table.

VEIL: Gentlemen, leave me alone now with . . . (*Half to herself*) with this old hummer.

BOOT: We'll go into the billiard room.

POLISH (*walking with the others past Lips*): Hurry, servants, bring us lights to the billiard room. (*Softly to Boot*) Lips is going to catch more than forty winks now!

(*Exits with friends and servants.*)

Scene 16

VEIL: They stamp by him — and he doesn't even budge. (*Approaching Lips*) Herr von Lips!

(*Lips snores loudly.*)

VEIL (*taken aback*): He snores — just like my first husband . . . a lovely habit! (*Louder*) Herr von Lips! Herr von Lips!

LIPS (*awakening with a start*): What is it . . .? Ah, Madame, it's you . . . excuse me.

VEIL: You snore . . . it's earthshaking.

LIPS: That comes from dreaming. I had a most amusing dream.

VEIL (*coquettish*): About me?

LIPS: Yes. You turned me down cold. (*Laughs.*)

VEIL: Is that amusing?

LIPS: In our dreams, everything seems different from reality.

VEIL: Yes, and they usually mean the opposite of reality. The fifteen minutes are up and . . .

LIPS (*absent-mindedly*): What fifteen minutes?

VEIL (*irritated*): The time to think over your proposal!

LIPS: Oh yes, I almost slept through it all. So you don't turn me down?

VEIL: You'd deserve it. However, this time I will . . .

LIPS: . . . forgive and forget because special circumstances . . . and so on and so forth. And so, since my dream has not come true, we'll keep on dreaming and talk about the future — that's another dream that seldom comes true. Please sit down.

VEIL: That's better than being stood up.

LIPS: When do you think we should announce our engagement?

VEIL: Well, since you have guests here tonight we might as well announce it now.

Scene 17

REDHOT (*entering from center, remaining in background, listening without being observed. In great excitement, to himself*):   There she is! The lamb facing the butcher.

LIPS: And when do you think the wedding should be?

VEIL: I leave it to you to set the date.

REDHOT (*to himself*):   What? The lamb submits to the butcher?

LIPS: We can be married in six weeks.

VEIL (*offended*):   Six weeks? I think if the bride has to make up her mind in fifteen minutes, the bridegroom could be ready within a week.

REDHOT (*disappointed*):   What's that? The lamb can hardly wait to be butchered?

LIPS (*in a daredevil mood*):   A week, you say? What for? It'd be too bad if we couldn't bring it off within twenty-four hours. The wedding will be tomorrow!

REDHOT (*rushing forward*):   And today will be the funeral!

LIPS: What do *you* want?

VEIL (*screaming*):   Redhot! (*Clasps a chair.*)

REDHOT: Yes, and at his redhottest!

LIPS: And she freezes!

REDHOT (*furiously to Lips*): Make your will, ecstasy-wrecker! Bliss-crusher!

VEIL: I'm lost!

LIPS: Not to me, you aren't. Do you think this dirty affair (*Pointing at Redhot*) makes any difference to me? Do you think I believed you were a pure soul? I wanted to do something foolish, and I see more and more that I couldn't have made a better choice. (*Embraces her.*)

REDHOT: Take your paws off her!

VEIL (*to Lips*): Call your servants!

LIPS: Why? I'll handle him myself!

REDHOT (*rolling up his sleeves*): Come on, if you have the grit!

LIPS: Windbag! I've had training in wrestling. (*Takes off his coat.*)

REDHOT (*clenching his fists*): But such a lesson you've never had! (*Both rush against each other and wrestle.*)

LIPS (*while wrestling*): You meaniac!

VEIL: But Herr von Lips . . . don't get mixed up in this . . . Help! Servants!

REDHOT (*pushing Lips toward the center left*): Servants won't do him any good!

LIPS (*gathering all his strength*): I'll show you that I don't need them! (*Pushes Redhot out the door.*)

VEIL: Isn't anyone here?

REDHOT (*coming back*): I'm here!

LIPS: What? You want more? Wait, you rat, I'll fix you! (*Pounces at Redhot. They wrestle, get close to and then onto the balcony, and fall off, still in a clutch, together with the loose railing.*)

VEIL (*screaming*): Oh no! (*Rushes to the balcony and looks down.*) Heavens . . . into the water! They're gone! Help! Help!

Scene 18

BOOT (*entering with guests and servants*):   Impossible . . .
   it can't be true . . .
POLISH: We could see it all from the billiard room.
VEIL: They've fallen into the river . . . both of them! (*Sinks
   into a chair.*)
BOOT: The killer, too?
POLISH: Quick! Boats! Boatmen!
GUESTS: Yes, boatmen, ropes, poles!

(*Guests leave center left.*)

Scene 19

BOOT (*to Veil*):   Brace yourself, dear!
VEIL: It's too much! A moment ago two men fought over
   me, and now their double death has made me a triple
   widow.
BOOT: Don't worry, Lips shall be saved. (*To Heel*) Come on,
   do something!
HEEL (*calmly*):   Jolly good show.
BOOT: Oh, you puddlebrain!

Scene 20

POLISH (*back with some guests*):   In the moonlight we saw
   a head bobbing in the water. The boatmen are rowing
   downstream.
BOOT: Let's look! (*All step onto the balcony.*)
POLISH: There — you see?

GUESTS: What? Where?
POLISH: There — don't you see?
BOOT: Nothing.
GUESTS: There's no chance.
BOOT: Murder, obviously.
POLISH: Lucky for the murderer that he drowned, too.

Scene 21

(*Lips has come back, drenched, through the left center, and heard the last remarks without being seen by the people on the balcony.*)

LIPS: Ah, but I haven't drowned . . . I still live . . . for the police, prison . . . horrible! (*Grabs his head with both hands in desperation.*)
GUESTS (*on the balcony*): No doubt — they're beyond help.
LIPS (*frantically*): I've got to run . . . to hide . . . quick . . .

(*Rushes out at side left.*)

CURTAIN

ACT TWO

(The granary of Peter Kraut's farm. Three trap-doors in the floor, a door right to the farmhouse, left to the fields. In the back a large door to the threshing floor, with large sheaves of grain. Table and chairs in the foreground.)

Scene 1

KRAUT *(to two farmhands)*: Is the clover cut?

FIRST FARMHAND: We'll do it today.

KRAUT: Is the fruit unloaded?

SECOND FARMHAND: We'll do it today.

KRAUT *(angrily)*: Today, today! You do everything today!

FIRST FARMHAND: We can leave it till tomorrow.

KRAUT: I'll wring your neck. It should've been done yester-day. The threshing must be done today, too. Aw, my head! I have to think of everything. Call the threshers, or I'll wring their necks, too.

FIRST FARMHAND: They're still eating breakfast.

(Farmhands leave.)

KRAUT *(to Kathy)*: And what about you? Cheer up, move, step lively!

KATHY *(sadly)*: How can I be lively when he is dead! *(Cries.)*

KRAUT: Now don't you overdo things, Kathy. You've cried

enough. When a godfather dies you cry the first hour, in the second you ask if he's left you anything, in the third you curse him because he hasn't, and in the fourth you go about your business as before.

KATHY: Oh, Uncle Kraut, you can't know how I feel — you've never seen him. He was such a fine person!

KRAUT: Why didn't he ever show his face here? I haven't the time to go visiting.

KATHY: He was so kind — he wouldn't hurt a fly.

KRAUT: He killed my pal. Redhot was my friend from the time when we were toddlers, but you don't see me blubbering all over the place.

THIRD FARMHAND (*comes from the left with a basketful of eggs*): Where do the eggs go?

KRAUT: Every time he asks the same question. (*Points to trapdoor.*) Down the hatch in the cellar, but careful. Did you lock the chickens in the coop?

THIRD FARMHAND: Not yet. I brought the eggs first.

KRAUT: No! Get back and hurry up. Ah, these fellows! They never know which comes first, the chicken or the egg!

THIRD FARMHAND (*puts down his basket without emptying it, mutters as he exits*): He won't let me hatch the eggs.

KRAUT (*to Kathy*): Come on, Kathy, fix my breakfast. I've got to put my papers in order, the Justice of the Will is going to show the farm to the heirs. I have to think of everything. Aw, my head!

(*Exits right.*)

Scene 2

KATHY (*alone*): In some moments I feel as if the whole world has died, and then again I think it's not possible, it couldn't have happened, he must be alive and all of a sudden I'll see him again.

LIPS (*disguised as a farmhand, cautiously from the left*): Psst! Kathy! Kathy!

KATHY (*frantically*): That was his voice!

LIPS (*stepping forward*): It's more than that — it's all of him.

KATHY (*jubilantly*): Is it possible . . . ? Yes . . . yes . . . you're alive! You didn't drown!

LIPS: The water spared me. I suppose I've been preserved for a higher destiny. (*Describes with his hand the motion of hanging.*)

KATHY: Oh, Herr von Lips! Hullo, Uncle . . . Herr von Lips is here!

LIPS: Hush, for heaven's sake . . . I'm a criminal!

KATHY: What?

LIPS: It's the truth. I'm doomed to the gallows.

KATHY: Why? Just because some silly people say you killed him on purpose . . .?

LIPS: There were witnesses. My friends saw everything from the billiard room. They opened the window just at the moment I shouted at Redhot, "Wait, you rat, I'll fix you!" This "Wait, you rat, I'll fix you!" seems to mean premeditated murder, and so this "Wait, you rat, I'll fix you!" will break my neck and becomes a terrible "Wait, you rat, I'll fix you!" for myself.

KATHY: Then I musn't tell Uncle?

LIPS: Not a word. To the world I'm drowned. My life depends on everybody believing that I'm giving the trout indigestion. But the worst of it is, I've run out of cash. This river trip was so unexpected, I didn't take any spending money along. These farm clothes took my last groschen.

KATHY: If only I still had the hundred thalers I owed you, but I gave them to Anton for you.

LIPS: Just goes to show the evil of being in too much of a hurry to pay back debts.

KATHY: Who saved you?

LIPS: *I* am the noble soul to whom I'm so deeply indebted. I swam ashore, but since I've been on dry land I've been in deep water.

KATHY: Lucky you have so many friends.

LIPS: I do have three I could almost trust. Once or twice I was about to get in touch with them . . . but that's my trouble — once I make up my mind I'm full of indecisions. I've fallen into the water, that's enough — I don't want to burn my fingers too, as everyone will who trusts his friends when he's down.

KATHY: I'm so glad you came here.

LIPS: But no word to anyone. I have to go abroad.

KATHY: Then you do have hopes for the future?

LIPS: Yes, but the future is tense and even more imperfect than the past. And I have to eat in the present! If I only had the money I often bangled on one stag dinner! I'm getting so hungry I wish I were a stag myself and could get my dinner from a bush.

KATHY: It's terrible to hear you talk like this. What can I do?

LIPS: Yes, it's ridiculous. I have an estate nearby; I haven't been there in years. If I could break in and take a sackful of silver — but no, my guards would catch me, and my own caretaker would throw me into jail.

KATHY: I wish I was rich. But I have nothing — not a groschen. What will you do now?

LIPS: Tell your uncle you know me. Tell him I'm some sort of a farmhand — er — that I was a helper of your mother's milkman. Put in a good word; maybe he'll hire me.

KATHY: What? You want to be a servant on your own farm?

LIPS: Don't forget, Kathy: I'm a criminal.

KATHY: But think what — (*Looking to the right*) — oh, here comes my uncle!

LIPS: Now talk to him, Kathy, talk!

Scene 3

KRAUT (*from the right*):   Aw, my head! Quick, Kathy, look after . . . (*Noticing Lips*) Who's that?

KATHY: It's . . . he is . . . well, that is . . .

LIPS (*coarsely*):   A farmhand.

KATHY: He'd like to work here.

KRAUT: I'm sick and tired of the workers I have. I don't need no new ones.

KATHY: But two ran away, yesterday.

KRAUT: Ah yes, you're right. I can't keep everything in my head.

KATHY: This one is so good, so honest . . .

KRAUT: How come you know him?

KATHY: I know him — yes — from the city.

KRAUT: From the city?

LIPS (*speaking like a peasant*):   I used to bring the milk.

KRAUT (*looking Lips over*):   You look clumsy to me. Do you know anything about farming? Say, can you plow?

LIPS: Plow? Do they put people to the plow here?

KRAUT: What kind of talk is that? Can you plant?

LIPS: I've played the field.

KRAUT: Have you done any sowing?

LIPS (*leering*):   Oh, in my youth I did plenty of sowing. But now, I'd say, I feel my corns more than my oats.

KRAUT: Did you have good crops?

LIPS: A bumper crop of sprouts.

KRAUT: Do you know how to make hay?

LIPS: In that, I'm an expert.

KRAUT: How about farm animals — pigs, cows?

LIPS: Pigs? I had no trouble bringing home the bacon. And cows? I used to work for a milkman.

KRAUT: But did you feed the cows in the pasture?

LIPS: Well, yes. We wanted them to get pasteurized.

KRAUT: Never heard of it. What kind of cows did you have?

LIPS: The very best. They gave nothing but cream.

KRAUT: Stop that twittle-twattle. Why not whipped cream?

LIPS: We didn't want to whip them; they might have turned sour on us. For ordinary milk we had ordinary cows.

KRAUT (*to Kathy*): I can't make head nor tail of him. (*To Lips*) Did you feed in the stable?

LIPS: No, we ate on the porch; in the stable we slept.

KRAUT: You're full of beans.

LIPS (*holding his stomach*): I wish I was.

KATHY: Give him his chance, Uncle Kraut. What he doesn't know he can pick up.

LIPS: That's true. I'm still young.

KRAUT: Aye, then; you are batty, but I'll give you a try. Help with the threshing. Then stack the hay . . . you know how to handle a pitchfork, don't you?

LIPS: Pitch me a breakfast, and I'll show you how I can handle a fork!

KRAUT: At my place we work first and eat afterward.

Scene 4

KRAUT (*to three farmhands entering left*): Well, it's time! Scuttle along, or I'll make mincemeat of you! (*The farmhands go to the threshing floor and start threshing.*)

KRAUT (*to Lips who hesitates*): Well? Waiting for a written invitation?

LIPS: Coming. Threshing probably helps a man to get rid of his cussedness. (*Goes to the floor and picks up a flail.*)

KATHY (*worried, to herself*): Hope he knows how.

KRAUT (*to Lips*): No, no! Not that way. You're holding the flail wrong side up!

LIPS: Isn't there any room for an individualist? (*Turns the flail around and begins to thresh with the others, ignoring their regular beat.*)

KRAUT (*to Kathy*):   Kathy, I don't think this fellow is going to work out. (*To Lips*) Not that way. Fall in with their beat.

LIPS (*to Kraut while threshing*):   You didn't give me the score. Why don't *they* follow *me?* (*Accidentally hits one farmhand on the head with the flail.*)

FIRST FARMHAND: Ow! He hit me!

KRAUT: Watch out, you chaffhead, and thrash the hay, not the heads!

LIPS (*coming to the front*):   I don't think I've hit upon an idea there!

FIRST FARMHAND (*to Kraut*):   This bogglehead can't handle a flail. He had better do something else — load the hay.

KRAUT: What? The hay isn't all in yet?

FIRST FARMHAND: We'll do it today!

KRAUT: Today! I'll chop you to pieces! Drop everything and bring in the hay while the sun is shining.

FARMHANDS: All right. Whatever you say. (*They leave.*)

KRAUT: Why must I think of everything . . . wait, I almost forgot. (*Calling Lips who is following the farmhands*) Hullo, you! Dummkopf!

LIPS (*turning around*):   What do you want?

KRAUT: At least you answer to your name.

LIPS: My name is Bob.

KRAUT: Run over to the courthouse and ask for the Justice . . .

LIPS (*scared*):   For who?

KRAUT: The Justice of the Will.

LIPS (*softly to Kathy*):   The word Justice gives me a tight feeling around my throat.

KRAUT: And ask him if he'll bring the gentlemen today.

LIPS: What gentlemen?

KRAUT: Never mind, do as you're told. (*To Kathy*) Take him
to the corner and show him the way to the courthouse.

LIPS (*softly to Kathy*): What if they recognize me there?
(*To Kraut*) It's awfully drafty in here . . . (*Takes a handkerchief from his pocket.*) I don't think your doors close
properly . . . (*Ties the handkerchief around his face.*)

KRAUT: Your health seems awfully delicate.

LIPS: I've got a toothache — my wisdom tooth is acting up.
(*To Kathy*) All right, Kathy, let's go to the courthouse.

(*Both leave.*)

Scene 5

KRAUT (*alone*): I've never seen a farmhand like him. I need
him like a hole in the . . . aw, my head!

REDHOT (*sticking his head from the haystack*): Psst! Kraut!
Pal!

KRAUT (*turning*): Eek! A head!

REDHOT: It's doomed, that head. Hide me, pal! (*Holds onto
Kraut.*)

KRAUT: I thought you got drowned.

REDHOT: Not I — Lips did.

KRAUT: Both of you, I thought . . .

REDHOT: The police know better, they're after me . . . I saw
a copper in every village. (*Suddenly screaming*) Ha! Here
they come! Help! Hide me!

KRAUT (*scared*): Who? Where?

REDHOT (*recovering*): No, it's nothing. I just thought . . .

KRAUT: You scared me to death . . . if you stabbed me now
I wouldn't give a drop of blood.

REDHOT: I've been scared that way all week. When I swam
ashore, I hid under a bush, and the Lips servants passed
by, inches away. "He's dead," they said. "Drowned. Mur-

dered." Since then the whole countryside is crawling with
coppers . . . they're looking high and low . . . to track me
down . . . I even think the unbelievable has happened . . .

KRAUT: What's that?

REDHOT: They put a price on my head.

KRAUT: Oh, the police don't throw away money like that.
Besides, it was just an accident. Why should anyone think
you meant to kill him?

REDHOT: It was a crime of passion. Besides, as a blacksmith,
I'm supposed to know better than leaving a railing on a
balcony, unfastened. (*Suddenly screaming*) Ha — there
they come! Handcuffs! Chains! Don't let 'em get me!
(*Clutches Kraut.*)

KRAUT (*scared*): What is it? Where?

REDHOT (*recovering*): Nothing. I just thought . . .

KRAUT: Listen, if you scare me once more like this . . .

REDHOT: Pal, you have no idea how it feels to have nothing
but fuzz in your head.

KRAUT: Where were you all week?

REDHOT: In the Vienna Woods but my tales are only of woe!
(*Startled*) Ha!

KRAUT (*also startled*): What?

REDHOT: Nothing. Last night I finally dared to come here.
You weren't home, so I crawled into the haystack and fell
asleep. Dreamed of nothing all night but coppers and tor-
tures . . . then the threshing woke me up.

KRAUT: And what now?

REDHOT: Hide me, pal . . .

KRAUT: But if . . .

REDHOT: You're my pal, you must hide me.

KRAUT: But where? Let me think . . . maybe in the bakery
. . . I'll not bake until the day after tomorrow . . .

REDHOT: Yes, yes, shove me into the oven. Even if they light
it, I won't rise. Nothing can be hotter than the fear of —

(*Screaming*) Ha, there! The hangman! (*Clutches Kraut again.*)

KRAUT (*freeing himself*): Stop that! How would a hangman get into my barn?

REDHOT: I can't help it. I'm so upset . . . if I'd calm down now, I'd get nervous. My mind's playing tricks . . . all of a sudden I see things . . . my knees give in . . . I give up. (*He sinks into Kraut's arms.*)

KRAUT (*holding him up*): Just wait until we are in the bakery.

REDHOT (*exhausted*): Carry me, pal . . . you're my pal . . . you must carry me . . .

KRAUT (*dragging Redhot out the door*): This has to happen to me . . . I don't know what to do first . . . and now you — aw, my head!

(*Both leave at right.*)

Scene 6

(*Kraut's living quarters. Right a cupboard, back left a bed enclosed by curtains. Doors left, right, and center. Table and chairs.*)

KATHY (*from the middle door, carrying milk and bread*): I made him a breakfast . . . not very fancy, but it's all I can give him. (*Puts the tray in the cupboard.*) Now I'll have to hurry and make the beds, get lunch, do the ironing . . . but I don't mind. It's all nothing now, since I know Herr von Lips is alive.

Scene 7

KRAUT (*from door, left, speaking back into the room he came from*): Now hush, I'll get you all you . . . (*Noticing Kathy*) What are you doing here?

KATHY: Tidying up a bit.

KRAUT: I don't need it tidy. You go now — uh — and see what happened to the new farmhand.

KATHY (*readily*): Yes, I'll go and meet him on his way back from the courthouse. (*Exits center.*)

KRAUT (*alone*):What a pest, that Redhot! If he wasn't my pal, I'd throw him out.

REDHOT'S VOICE (*from inside, left*): Bring me some food, pal, I'm starving!

KRAUT: Aye, aye! (*Taking a plate with leg of lamb and some bread from the cupboard, he takes it through the door, left. Speaking inside*) There, eat your fill! (*Returning to the stage, but still speaking back*) And take it easy till I come back. (*Closes the door.*) If anyone finds out that I'm hiding a killer . . . !

REDHOT'S VOICE: Bring me something to drink, pal!

KRAUT: Just a moment, and keep your voice down! (*Takes a bottle of wine from the cupboard.*) You'd think he was dying of thirst! (*Exits left, speaking inside*) Now eat and drink, and tush! (*Coming back, speaking back*) Or someone will find out about you! (*Closes the door.*) What a house-guest! (*Wipes his brow.*)

REDHOT'S VOICE: A pillow, pal, bring me a pillow!

KRAUT (*wringing his hands*): What next? (*Takes a pillow from his bed.*) Why can't he lie down on the oven bench? (*Exits left, speaking inside*) There you are, but one more peep out of you, and, I swear, I'll call the coppers and turn you in! (*Comes out and closes the door.*) There couldn't be more fuss if someone had triplets here . . . aw, my head!

(*Exits right.*)

Scene 8

KATHY (*entering with Lips from the middle*): You really must be tired. You're used to walking on carpets and traveling in carriages . . . and now . . .

LIPS: If I could only get hold of those poets who call a meadow a flowery carpet and a lawn a lush green velvet . . . if only I could chase those lyrical nitwits in their bare feet for three hours all over their touted nature . . . I would let it cost me a pretty groschen!

KATHY (*taking the milk and bread from the cupboard and putting them on the table*): At least you must have worked up an appetite!

LIPS: What's that you've got there?

KATHY: Bread and milk.

LIPS: No rolls?

KATHY: That's our best bread.

LIPS: And your only brand of coffee is milk?

KATHY: I wish I could serve you sweet rolls and eggs . . .

LIPS: Oh, you sweet Kathy, you! You're such a sweet Kathy that this breakfast, served by your hand, reminds me of the most delicious hangman's meal . . .

KATHY: You must feel terrible.

LIPS: Well, yes and no. I've had an easy life for so long that I developed a craving for a little excitement. But a full week of excitement is more than I had bargained for. And there's still more to come. Then there's something else . . .

KATHY (*sympathetically*): What's that? You can tell me everything, Herr von Lips.

LIPS: Oh, you sweet Kathy, you, you're getting sweeter by the minute.

KATHY: But Herr von Lips . . .

LIPS: A sip of milk, that will cool me off. (*Eats and drinks while continuing to talk.*) You wouldn't understand if I told you. You have never killed anyone, have you?

KATHY: Good Lord, what an idea!

LIPS: Well . . . I meant . . . if, for instance, someone had killed himself because he was in love with you, you'd be an indirect murderess.

KATHY: Thank heaven, I'm not such a man-killing beauty.

LIPS: Oh, Kathy, you don't know what a sweet Kathy you are! (*Embraces her.*)

KATHY (*freeing herself*):   Oh, please . . .

LIPS: Quick, a sip of milk. (*Drinks.*) So, I'm a good boy again. What I meant to say to you . . . I have hallucinations.

KATHY: Ha - lucy - . . . what?

LIPS: They are fantasies that form in the empty spaces of our brains, and sometimes they step out — scarecrows that have come alive on the fields of our loneliness. They roll their lifeless eyes, show their grisly teeth, and draw their skeleton hands to threaten us with a musty slap in the face — that's hallucinations.

KATHY: Oh my, city folks get into the darndest pickles!

LIPS: When it gets dark I see white ghosts . . .

KATHY: How can you? At night, all cows are black.

LIPS: It's silly of me . . . I didn't drown him on purpose. And yet . . . always that snow-white blacksmith! You don't know how unnerving a white blacksmith can be!

KATHY: You just have to forget about him.

LIPS: Even this milk reminds me . . . if it were only a bit coffee brown! I hate white! (*Pushes the glass away so that some milk spills on the table.*)

Scene 9

KRAUT (*entering with ink and quills from the right*):   What's the idea, slopping milk all over the table?

LIPS: I've had breakfast.

KRAUT: My farmhands eat on the porch. (*To Kathy*) Why do you let this fellow eat here?

KATHY: He has a bad tooth.

KRAUT: Why don't you wrap him up in cotton, the poor darling?

KATHY (*wiping the table*): There. It's all cleaned up.

KRAUT: Take off the milk, make room for the ink. (*Puts writing material on the table.*)

LIPS: The clerk in the courthouse said the men will be here soon with the Justice of the Will.

KRAUT: Oh? Come on, then, Kathy . . . let's meet them.

KATHY: Meet who?

KRAUT: The lucky heirs of the dead Lips.

LIPS (*shouting, startled*): The dead . . . ?

KRAUT: Well, yes, what are you hollering about?

LIPS: I can't get used to Lips being dead. He was such a fine man.

KATHY: A real gentleman!

LIPS: It's too bad.

KRAUT: Oh, fiddlesticks . . . one bufflehead less in this world. No one will miss him.

LIPS: But he was . . .

KRAUT: Shut up. I know better what he was . . . a cracked pot, with holes besides. He didn't know what he wanted.

LIPS: He felt empty inside.

KRAUT: That's not true . . . he was full of hot air, everyone knows that. Come, Kathy! And you (*To Lips*) stay here and see if the gentlemen need anything.

Scene 10

LIPS (*alone*): That's a fine thing, how he talks about me. And I have to listen and pretend I'm not I. That takes some

pretending, all right. But there are many situations where
pretending is quite a feat.

Song

Your boss throws a party, invites you to come.
You go, for you know where your gravy comes from.
There's Mrs., there's Grandma, there's Junior and Sis . . .
The wine is not aged, but the Mrs. sure is;
You wish that the beer were as cold as the steak,
And the jokes not as stale as the strawberry cake.
The Sis plays piano, and Junior, French horn,
By the time you escape, it is three in the morn.
You say: "Folks, you were charming, your eats were a treat . . ."
    To pretend in this way is a fabulous feat.

"Your wife has a lover," so says your best friend.
"Confess, shameless hussy, prepare for the end!
Confess, or I'll wallop the tar out of you!"
That's what you would say, feeling mad as you do.
But easy! Find out, before raising the roof,
Or you are the fool when she asks for the proof.
She comes in, all dolled up, and says, "Now I must run
To visit Eileen!" You say, "Darling, have fun,
Just give me a kiss, you look fetching, look sweet . . ."
    To pretend in this way is a fabulous feat.

A man with a corn on each one of his toes
Takes a girl to a dance and intends to propose.
She is rich, she is pretty, her figure's divine
But her manner of dancing is elephantine.
She's far more on *his* feet than she is on *hers*
But he smiles at her bravely every time this occurs.
"Your dance is divine and it makes life complete!"
    To pretend in this way shows two fabulous feet.

Encore

They now have a bomb that more damage can do
Than all bombs together in World War II.
They can poison the air now with horrible stuff,
It's paid for by taxes, and it's never enough.
Populations increase at an ominous rate,
All mankind seems bound for a terrible fate.
And yet, we live on, as if nothing were wrong,
We laugh and rejoice in wine, women, and song;
We go to a show and relax in our seat . . .
  To pretend in this way is a fabulous feat.

(*Exits right.*)

Scene 11

KRAUT (*guiding the Justice, Boot, Heel, and Polish into the room*): This is the farmhouse, my living quarters . . .

HEEL (*looking around*): A nice hunting ground for a legacy.

JUSTICE OF THE WILL: After due inspection of the country house, the rightful heirs in pleno titulo will proceed now to a thorough examination of the present estate of this leased property.

KRAUT: Hullo, Bob!

LIPS (*with handkerchief tied around his face, from the right, with disguised voice*): What is it?

KRAUT: Move the table over here and bring a few chairs. (*Lips does so with Kraut's and Kathy's help.*)

POLISH: I must say, such a farm isn't bad!

HEEL: Smashing!

JUSTICE: Lessee Peter Kraut, you are herewith directed, by order of the court, to pay henceforth the monthly sum stipulated in the rental contract to the new owners in titulo, Messieurs Boot, Heel, and Polish. (*Pulls out a paper scroll, shows it to Kraut and places it on the table.*) Kindly peruse paragraph 1, section 1, stipulation 1, of this duly filed testamentum.

POLISH (*to Boot and Heel*): I'm not sorry Lips got drowned.

BOOT: Neither am I.

HEEL: Jolly good thing the bloody fool's gone.

BOOT: A suitable epitaph for him would be: He was too dumb for this world.

POLISH: It was hard to put up with his rubbish — but it paid off!

LIPS (*softly to Kathy*): My ears are getting a heart attack!

KATHY (*softly to Lips*): And to these men you left your fortune?

LIPS (*softly to Kathy*): Everything. It was on the day I wanted to shoot myself.

KRAUT (*to Lips*): Take that rag off your face.

LIPS: I can't — my wisdom tooth gets stupider all the time.

POLISH: Come on! Let's have a look around! (*Wants to open the door left and finds it locked.*)

KRAUT (*embarrassed*): I must have left the key downstairs. Will you gentlemen look at the rest of the farm in the meantime? Kathy, you show them around while I get the key.

BOOT: Yes, blue-eyes, show us the way . . .

JUSTICE: If it pleases the heirs in titulo . . .

LIPS (*to himself*): Scoundrels!

JUSTICE: . . . to pervestigate the property in question . . .

POLISH: All right. Let's have a look at the farm!

    (*Boot, Heel, and Polish, the Justice, and Kathy
    leave through center.*)

KRAUT (*calling after them*): I'll be with you in a moment!
    (*To Lips*) Well, stop the dilly-dallying and get moving!

LIPS (*hesitantly*): I only want to . . .

KRAUT: Go on, stay with the visitors!

(*Lips exits center.*)

KRAUT (*alone*): Now what do I do with my Redhot guest? (*Unlocking door, left*) One thing I know — if I get to be born again, no more pals!

(*Exits left.*)

Scene 12

LIPS (*peering cautiously from the center*): Everybody's gone — good. (*Coming forth*) So that's how heirs do their mourning for their dear departed! But I'm not quite as dead as you think, my dear friends! (*Sits down and writes on the back of the testament left on the table.*) I'll add a little surprise for you, just because you're such dear friends. There! Dated June 19. I "drowned" on the twentieth, so I still was a citizen on the nineteenth, with all my rights. Now my signature. There . . . (*Getting up*) that'll do it!

(*Hurries out through the center.*)

Scene 13

KRAUT (*from the left, talking back into the room*): Come on, quick, I have to hide you somewhere else . . .

REDHOT (*entering with large leg of lamb, wine, and pillow. He is swaggering*): But, pal . . .

KRAUT: Hurry up, they may come back at any moment.

REDHOT: You don't think this teeny bottle and that child's helping of meat will last me all day?

KRAUT: I'll get you more, don't worry.

REDHOT: For a pal, nothing is too much.

KRAUT: Now listen. In my granary, where I found you this morning, there are three trapdoors in the floor. It makes no difference which one you take, they all lead into the cellar.

REDHOT: That's too complicated. You come and show me.

KRAUT (*angrily*):   But I have to be with my guests . . . don't make such a fuss.

REDHOT: Don't feel that way about a pal. And in the cellar it will be cold — I'd better take along a few things. (*Takes blankets, a nightcap, and two pillows from Kraut's bed.*)

KRAUT: Hold it! You're taking my entire bed along!

REDHOT: You'll get along. For a pal you have to show a little hospitality.

KRAUT: Now go on, move!

REDHOT (*muttering to himself*):   Come on, Kraut, old pal, don't be such a sour Kraut!

(*Both leave.*)

Scene 14

BOOT (*coming back with Heel, Polish, Justice, and Lips*):   And I tell you, I'm not going to become a country yokel just because I inherited a farm. I'll sell it!

HEEL: I'll keep it as a hunting ground.

POLISH: Now just a minute. I have a say here, too, I don't like people who make my mind up for me.

BOOT: Let's vote!

HEEL: Righto!

POLISH: I'll show you a thing or two!

BOOT: You won't show us even half a thing. Understand?

JUSTICE: If the rightful heirs in titulo will permit me . . .

POLISH: You shut up!

JUSTICE: Perhaps the point in question is decided by a paragraphus testamenti.

POLISH: All right, check if you want, but I tell you right away . . .

Scene 15

KRAUT (*from the left*):   Here's the key now.

JUSTICE: Hm, strange, I never noticed this clause before . . .

KRAUT: If you wish to inspect the room, I can open it now.

JUSTICE (*shaking his head*):   Hm . . . hm!

POLISH: What's the meaning of this legal humphing?

JUSTICE: This amounts to an outright cancellation of the will.

BOOT, HEEL, POLISH, KRAUT: Cancellation?

JUSTICE: Authentic handwriting of the departed . . . signed June 19 . . . everything's valid. (*Reads*) "Since I am disgusted with the world, and with my friends in particular, I herewith declare this will null and void, and name as the sole heir of all my property, cash, as well as estates and appurtenances, the niece of my tenant Peter Kraut — Miss Katherine Kraut."

KRAUT (*shouting in surprise*):   Kathy?

BOOT, HEEL, AND POLISH: What Kathy?

KRAUT: Kathy ! ! !

(*General surprise while Lips sneaks off to the back, smiling.*)

CURTAIN

ACT THREE

(Kraut's living quarters, as at the end of Act Two)

Scene 1

(The same group of surprised persons are assembled as at the end of Act Two.)

BOOT, HEEL, POLISH, AND KRAUT: Kathy!

HEEL *(to Justice)*:   Can't we contest the will?

JUSTICE *(shrugging)*:   You may contest, but . . .

POLISH: . . . the only winner would be the lawyer.

JUSTICE: The cancellation is legally valid.

KRAUT: And the Justice is a man who knows. My Kathy is sole heir.

BOOT *(to himself)*:   The girl's pretty, very pretty . . . If I succeed . . .

HEEL *(to himself)*:   If I make her my lady . . .

POLISH *(to himself)*:   If I try, Kathy plus inheritance could be mine!

KRAUT *(to himself)*:   Many uncles have married their nieces!

JUSTICE *(to himself)*:   And last winter I had to be fool enough to take my third wife!

KRAUT: Well, first of all we have to tell Kathy the good news . . .

80

LIPS (*in the background, to himself*): Now we'll hear what we'll hear. (*Hides behind the bed curtain.*)

KRAUT (*calling at the door, right*): Kathy!

Scene 2

KATHY (*carrying a tray with wine and glasses*): Here I am, Uncle. (*Puts the tray on the table.*)

HEEL: My fair lady!

BOOT: Hello, dolly!

POLISH: Funny girl!

KRAUT: Kiss me, Kate!

KATHY (*pointing at the glasses*): May I help you . . . ?

BOOT: From your hand, every drink is nectar!

KATHY: Nectar? That's a grape we don't grow around here.

POLISH (*taking her hand*): Pretty hand. (*Holds it next to his.*) Go well together, don't they?

HEEL (*stepping up to Kathy*): Miss Kitty . . .

POLISH (*crowding Heel away*): Why don't you go to London?

BOOT: Kathy, my child, let me tell you. What you need is a protector, a man of experience. Not a young squirt who's just trying to impress you. Take me, for instance: I'm forty-five — the forties are the best age for a man.

KRAUT (*flirting with Kathy*): I'm even better — I'm forty-seven.

KATHY (*to Kraut*): What's the matter with them? They roll their eyes like sick calves.

JUSTICE: They wish to congratulate the very charming rightful pleno titulo heiress of the departed Herr von Lips.

KATHY: Who's an heiress?

KRAUT: You, Kathy, you're the sole heiress!

KATHY (*delighted*): His heiress? He made me his heiress?

How clever of him . . . then the money is safe . . . oh, this makes me so happy!

KRAUT: And I'm happy with you, now and forever, apple of my eye. This clause to his will — why it's a regular Santa Claus!

KATHY (*excited*): Where is — er — Bob?

BOOT, HEEL, POLISH (*taken aback*): Bob?

KRAUT (*angrily*): What about Bob? Are you . . .

KATHY: I've got to talk to him.

KRAUT: I had that notion before . . . Kathy, don't you dare be in love with that fellow.

BOOT: Where is that wretch?

HEEL (*swinging his riding crop*): Here's a medicine that'll cure his love!

KRAUT: Where is he hiding? (*They move toward the door.*)

KATHY (*suddenly frightened*): Hiding? (*With sudden decision*) No, no, you needn't look for him.

POLISH (*coming back*): I'd rather look at you any time, honey.

KATHY (*eagerly*): That's right, look at me. Stay right here.

BOOT (*coming from the door*): Then you're not in love with that Bob?

KATHY (*to herself*): The main thing is to keep them off Herr von Lips' back. (*Aloud*) What gives you that idea?

BOOT: You were in such a hurry to tell him . . .

KATHY: Do I have to be in love with every Bob, Dick, and Harry if I want to tell him something?

POLISH: Then you are not . . .

KRAUT: Your heart isn't Bobbing, then?

KATHY: Of course not. Why should it be?

BOOT: Absurd . . . you and that bumpkin!

KATHY: Ridiculous, isn't it?

KRAUT: That monkey shuffle . . . he never looks you in the eye!

HEEL: A mouth like a bullfrog . . .

POLISH: All thumbs and two left legs . . .

KATHY: Don't you think I noticed all that? Do you think I'd go for that?

BOOT AND HEEL (*crowding about her*):   Forgive me, child!

POLISH (*trying to cut in*):   My Dulcinea!

KRAUT: Apple of my eye!

KATHY: You're all forgiven!

BOOT: Then I do have hope?

POLISH (*crowding around Kathy*):   Let's go for a buggyride, just you and me.

HEEL (*also crowding*):   You must come and see my etchings!

KATHY: Gentlemen! Please! I'll make my choice when the time comes.

KRAUT: Kathy . . . you won't be ungrateful and forget what I've done for you?

KATHY: No, Uncle, I won't forget a thing.

KRAUT (*tenderly*):   Then may I send the others away?

KATHY (*relieved*):   Oh, yes, please send them away. And we . . . we'll talk about it later, Uncle Kraut. (*Runs away through center.*)

KRAUT (*happily holding his head with both hands*):   Oh, you luckiest of all cabbage heads!

BOOT: What was that?

POLISH: No — it can't be!

HEEL: Miss Kitty!

(*All three leave, running after Kathy.*)

JUSTICE: I wonder if they'll get anywhere, the pleno titulo ex-heirs.

(*Exits, running after them.*)

Scene 3

KRAUT (*alone*): If they only don't change her mind — I won't let her out of my sight! (*Attempts to leave.*)

LIPS (*jumping from his hiding place, holding Kraut by the coat tails*): Stop! You stay here!

KRAUT (*screaming in surprise*): Ah! (*Recognizing "Bob"*) Oh, it's you! Let me go, or you'll catch it!

LIPS (*very excited*): I already caught it! (*Holding Kraut*) And I won't let it get away!

KRAUT (*trying to free himself*): How dare you touch me?

LIPS: How dare you get married?

KRAUT: I tell you for your own good . . .

LIPS: And I tell you for your own harm . . .

KRAUT: You have the gall to threaten . . . ?

LIPS: You have the gall to love?

KRAUT: That's none of your business!

LIPS: Marry? An old dodderer like you?

KRAUT: I'm a man in his best years.

LIPS (*grimly*): We'll see about that! (*Rolls up his sleeves.*)

KRAUT (*getting worried, to himself*): He's out of his mind . . . (*In a friendly voice while trying to get to the door*) Now wait a minute, Bob, listen . . .

LIPS (*cutting off his retreat*): That's it, leaseholder! Your lease on life is over!

KRAUT (*getting more scared*): Bob . . . come on . . . be sensible! You wouldn't want to beat up an old man?

LIPS: My, how quickly you have aged! Why, you strong groom, you man in his best years! This is your worst year for it's your last!

KRAUT: Aw, my head! Come on, Bob . . . we can talk things over.

LIPS: You will not marry Kathy!

KRAUT (*very meekly*): Just as you say, Bob. Let someone else marry her!

LIPS: No! The others mustn't marry her, either.

KRAUT: You know what? Throw them out, those others.

LIPS: It's your house . . . You throw them out!

KRAUT: I'll tell them you ordered it.

LIPS: Good.

KRAUT: See? I do everything you want. Now let me go . . . how else can I throw them out?

LIPS: All right, disappear! (*Pushes him out the door.*) You have to show those clods.

KRAUT (*sticking his head through the door*): Anything else you want? Just tell me.

LIPS (*brusquely*): No, that's all.

KRAUT (*showing his irony*): See, Bob? I do just what you want. (*Withdraws his head.*)

Scene 4

LIPS (*alone*): I believe he's making a fool of me . . . it doesn't matter. I'm doing a good job of making a fool of myself. I'm having bad luck with my heirs: Kathy talks about me just like the others — monkey shuffle, bullfrog mouth, two left legs — by God, next time I die I'll leave everything to the deaf and dumb . . . they can't slander me. But, come to think of it, there must be slanderers and crooks around, too. If everyone were the same as everyone else, the world would really be a bore!

SONG

A man sits at home, with no life and no pep,
He lazes around and he won't walk a step.
Even mailing a letter he thinks is a chore,
It's too much exertion to open the door.

Another man climbs every mountain in sight,
To hike thirty miles is his greatest delight,
And when he's all in and his tongue's hanging out,
Why, then he feels good, like a freshwater trout.
I say this to show what I always have found:
  There are all kinds of different people around.

At election time someone is raising his voice
To praise good old George as the man of his choice.
"A man of the people, as smart as a fox,
As sound as a dollar, and sturdy as rocks."
A second man shouts: "Your old George is a fink,
A fuzzy, soft-headed, pseudo-liberal pink."
A third man thinks George is a tool of the rich,
A right-wing extremist, a son of a witch.
A fourth believes George is on safe middle-ground!
  There are all sorts of different people around.

A gal thinks she's fat, does not know what to do,
Her size: 39 — 36 — 42.
She worries, she diets, she cries and she frets,
And the worser she feels, why, the fatter she gets.
One sees her at dances but not with a him.
She's fat, but her chances for marriage are slim.
But one day a man calls: "This gal makes me jump!
She is so delightfully rounded and plump!"
Pretty soon they're hitched up and honeymoon-bound . . .
  What luck, there are different people around!

Scene 5

(*The granary, as at the beginning of Act Two. It is
evening. Kathy enters from the right, holding a
lantern.*)

KATHY: My godfather disappeared, and those city slickers keep pestering me. Maybe I'll be safe from them here. (*Places the lantern on the table.*) Uh-uh, someone's coming. (*Steps back into the shadow.*)

Scene 6

LIPS (*entering from the left, without noticing Kathy*): I don't want to stay and I can't leave, I'm in hot water no matter where I go.

KATHY: Herr von Lips . . . at last I've found you!

LIPS: Oh, it's you.

KATHY: That was smart of you, taking the money away from those hogs.

LIPS (*coldly*): I'm glad you find it smart. It's a real compliment.

KATHY (*not noticing his coldness*): I'll have to tell you my plan.

LIPS (*coldly*): That's right, tell me your plan. Tell me that Uncle Kraut looks like a man whom one might, half from inclination, half from gratitude, take for the real thing . . . and after all, you're used to living in his house . . . come on, tell me.

KATHY (*taken aback*): What makes you think I want to marry Uncle Kraut? He's like a father to me.

LIPS: Oh, then it's a young man! Come on, tell me. Is he in the army? Does he have to buy his way out? You are the heiress, you have the cash. Or has he run away, and wants you to join him? Marriage abroad? In the United States, maybe? You can travel first class, the money is yours!

KATHY: So you think I'm in love with a young whippersnapper? (*Looks at Lips and shakes her head.*)

LIPS: Not an old and not a young one? But you said you had a plan?

KATHY: Oh, I do have a plan. I'll take all your cash and sell all your property, stick the money in a fat envelope, and send it to you abroad so you can live in comfort . . . that's my plan.

LIPS (*in happy surprise*): Kathy . . . is this what you want to do? But . . . (*Calming down*) whom are you going to marry?

KATHY: No one.

LIPS: You don't care for anybody?

(*Kathy is about to say something, but keeps silent.*)

LIPS: Has every man a mouth like a bullfrog and does the entire male population shuffle along on two left legs?

KATHY: Oh, you listened when we called you names! But you must have noticed that I did it only to protect you.

LIPS: You did? Yes, I believe you did . . . but I didn't notice!

KATHY: There are quite a few things you don't notice.

LIPS (*looking at her while she keeps smiling at him*): Well, I really think I've been blind as a bat, and living upside down to match. (*Steps toward her, then checks himself.*) Kathy . . . I don't have the courage . . . at my age, it's too easy to stub one's toe and too painful to admit it. Yet, Kathy . . .

Scene 7

BOOT (*rushing in with Heel and Polish from the left*): Here he is, the impertinent lout . . .

POLISH: Kraut gave us your message . . .

HEEL: Throw us out — eh? You?

JUSTICE (*coming in*): Gentlemen! Gentlemen!

BOOT (*to Lips*): We'll teach you a lesson . . .

POLISH: A one-two Spanish step . . .

HEEL: And our riding crop will be the castanets.

BOOT: So, you miserable . . . (*Grabs Lips by the collar and recognizes him.*) Oh ! ! !

POLISH (*coming close*): What is it? (*Recognizes Lips.*) Oh ! ! !

BOOT: Friend Lips . . . ?

HEEL AND POLISH: You're alive?

LIPS: Yes, I'm alive, you double-crossing dirty skunks!

BOOT: Forgive us . . .

HEEL: We couldn't know . . .

POLISH: A thoughtless word . . .

JUSTICE (*amazed*): Lipsius redivivus! Permit me to ascertain the identity of the corpus delicti.

LIPS: Leave me alone! I want to wash my hands of the whole world and its crooks and backslappers — I'm going to retire to a beautiful secluded spot.

JUSTICE: Secluded, that's possible . . . but beautiful? I doubt it.

LIPS: What do you mean?

JUSTICE: I am referring to the charge of the alleged blacksmith murder still pending before the courts. For this reason I am forced to take precautionary measures to ascertain the availability of your esteemed persona suspecta.

LIPS: You'd dare?

JUSTICE: Merely acting upon superior instructions in accordance with my obligatio officialis.

LIPS: Redhot drowned by chance. I'm innocent.

JUSTICE: Quod erit demonstrandum by decision without prejudice by the properly authorized court. In view of the established motive, id est, a rivalry over a contested female, and the threatening utterings overheard by corroborating witnesses, the absence of premeditation will have to be proved by evidentia conclusiva.

LIPS: Kathy — I knew it! I'm lost!

JUSTICE (*calling at the door*):   Holla, servants, call the police, the magistratus populi.

KATHY (*to Lips*):   My God — what can I do now?

JUSTICE (*locking the doors and putting the keys into his pocket*):   I'll lock the doors and the farmhands will stand guard. Escape is impossible.

KATHY (*softly to Lips*):   I'll tell Uncle Kraut who you are. He must save you! (*Runs out at the left.*)

JUSTICE (*to Lips*):   Habeo corpus, and I am going to keep it. My deepest respect! (*Bows deeply before Lips and leaves with the others, at left. One hears the door being locked.*)

Scene 8

LIPS (*alone, as if waking from a dream*):   How could this be? I was so happy . . . I didn't even bother counting what number cloud I was on. Only a moment ago my hopes were soaring . . . and now I'm down, locked in. The contrasts are too great . . . paradise and prison . . . dear Kathy and the dungeon . . . love and a death cell . . . these are the hot-and-cold Turkish-bath showers of my mind. It's dark and I'm shivering: light and warmth always run out together on the fugitive. The conscience of a criminal is a night owl . . . during the day it dozes, but in the dark its eyes grow sharp . . . it sees someone in every corner. (*Looking around, staring at a corner*) Over there! Isn't that . . . ? No, it's just a rake . . . and I thought it was Redhot's ghost, ready to rake me over the coals of hell. If people knew what it means to drown a blacksmith, nobody would even try. Now the lantern flickers, gets dim . . . that's just what I need! (*Holds up the lantern and walks across the stage, tripping over the handle of a trapdoor.*) Uh-uh . . . what's this? (*Shines the light on the floor.*) An iron ring . . . a bad omen for a candidate for the

chaingang! (*Examines the ring.*) But this is . . . (*Pulling*)
yes, it's a trapdoor . . . to the cellar. Maybe I can hide . . .
barrels, sacks . . . they'll search in vain . . . Kathy at mid-
night . . . perhaps a secret passage . . . escape . . . freedom!
It opens up the thrill of a penny-dreadful . . . (*Opens the
trapdoor in the center of the stage.*) It looks scary . . . but
what do I have to lose? (*Climbs down, holding his lantern.
Gloomy music from the orchestra.*)

Scene 9

Lips (*from downstairs, screaming*): Ah ! ! !
Redhot (*also downstairs*): Ah ! ! !
Lips (*still downstairs*): Specter of hell!
Redhot (*downstairs*): Satan!
Lips (*climbing up, holding the lantern*): Help! Help! (*Shuts
the trapdoor.*) His ghost is down there . . . I've never seen
it so clearly before!
Redhot (*opening the trapdoor. Only visible to his chest. He is
wrapped in Kraut's bed cover and wearing his nightcap*):
His ghost is after me! Air! Air!
Lips: His shade rises up . . . down with you! (*Runs to the
trapdoor and steps on it, pushing down Redhot.*) Wait,
netherworld, I'll teach you to send up specters! Isn't the
world up here ghastly enough?
Redhot (*emerging from the trapdoor, left*): The horror's kill-
ing me! I can't breathe!
Lips: What? Another one? Infernal apparition! (*Runs to the
trapdoor left and steps on it.*) I've killed only one — why
this horrible multiplication?
Redhot (*pushes up the trapdoor in the middle*): I've got to
come up for air . . .
Lips (*beside himself*): Down with you! What's dead belongs

under the earth. (*Throws himself on the trapdoor and presses Redhot down.*) The whole ground is undermined, the blacksmiths shoot up like weeds! It's too much ... I can't stand it! (*Trying to get up*) My knees ... my heart ... I have no strength left! (*Collapses. Voices are heard from outside, "Long live Herr von Lips!" The music ends.*)

LIPS: What's that? (*Voices closer, "Long live Herr von Lips!"*) Live? How can I live? I'm too busy dying. (*Raises himself with effort. The door left is being unlocked.*)

Scene 10

KRAUT (*rushing in with Kathy, Boot, Heel, Polish, Justice of the Will and several farmers. Happily excited*): Aw, my head! Do I have one? Don't I? Do I have a landlord? Don't I?

KATHY (*pointing at Lips*): There he is!

JUSTICE (*to Kraut*): You're aiding and abetting a criminal, letting your people cheer!

KRAUT (*paying no attention to him*): And I ... miserable baboon that I am ... permit me, Herr von Lips, to have you carried to your home in conscience-stricken triumph.

JUSTICE (*stepping between them*): Cease and desist! Herr von Lips belongs to the court's justitia.

KRAUT: He's innocent ... I can prove it.

JUSTICE: How? Redhot is dead!

Scene 11

REDHOT (*coming up the trapdoor at right*): Says who? Herr von Lips is dead!

KRAUT: Says who? Herr von Lips is alive!

REDHOT: Shut up! (*To Justice*) Take me away, I'd rather be in prison than buried alive!

LIPS (*watching Redhot in happy amazement*): Redhot? Is it really you? You are alive?

REDHOT (*equally amazed*): Herr von Lips? You? You are not dead?

LIPS (*offering him his hand*): Not at all, my dear victim!

REDHOT (*taking the hand*): Neither am I, my dear corpse!

JUSTICE: Neither one is dead, the casus dissolves into nothing.

BOOT (*approaching Lips ingratiatingly*): I hope you won't refuse our most sincere wishes for your future happiness.

LIPS: On the contrary . . . you can contribute very much to it.

BOOT, HEEL, POLISH (*eagerly*): How? Tell us!

LIPS: Jump off the balcony — and drown yourselves, but good!

JUSTICE: Touché!

(*Boot, Heel, and Polish withdraw in confusion.*)

LIPS (*to Redhot*): I'm no longer your rival. Take your Mathilda and I'll throw in an ample dowry.

REDHOT: I'll take the dowry and buy myself a blacksmith shop . . . but the widow — no, thanks. I've lost all my passion for Mathilda.

LIPS: And I've developed a passion for Kathy. Now I see that I truly was a man full of nothing . . . I had no purpose, life had no meaning — I was really empty inside. I was only half a man because the better half was missing! But now I've found it, better late than never. Come here, Kathy, let me call you by my last name — from now on, you'll get Lips' service for life! (*Embraces and kisses her.*)

ALL: Three cheers for the groom and bride! (*Everyone cheers.*)

CURTAIN

The Talisman

(DER TALISMAN)

A Farce with Songs, in Three Acts

The Talisman (*Der Talisman*) gave Nestroy, as Titus (center), the opportunity to play, with the help of several wigs, a redhead, a blond, a blacktop, and a prematurely gray-haired man. He performed the role 112 times, from the first showing, December 16, 1840, until 1860, two years before his death. Costume study from the Vienna Theaterzeitung.

Today, the appeal of *The Talisman* has shifted to Nestroy's sarcastic scrutiny of human prejudice. His irony is all the more accepted, since it is directed against a prejudice (against redheads) that no longer exists. The play has been widely acclaimed by postwar audiences in Austria and Germany. The scene above, from a performance at the Landestheater, Hannover, shows Titus (extreme right) just before his final realization that the worst prejudice can be overcome by money, represented in this case by a rich uncle (second from right).

CHARACTERS

Titus, an unemployed barber's helper
Salome, the village gooseherd
Lady Cypressa, a wealthy author
Emma, her daughter
Constantia, her lady's maid
Flora, her chief gardener
Poponseed, Flora's helper
Monsieur Marquis
George, servant of Lady Cypressa
Sponge, guest of Lady Cypressa
Bung, beer salesman and uncle of Titus
Notary, guests, servants, peasants,
    peasant boys and girls, a policeman

Time and place: Mid-nineteenth-century Austria

ACT ONE

(*A village square. In the background a well and two stone benches. Left, a garden wall with a gate leading to the garden of Lady Cypressa.*)

Scene 1

(*Several country boys and girls. Dance music offstage.*)

FIRST BOY (*to a girl*):   The band has started. Let's go.

SECOND BOY (*to another girl*):   You and me—we've been waltzing together at these village fairs for ten years.

GIRL (*to a boy*):   I wouldn't dance with anyone in the world but you.

(*They all pair off except third boy, a very ugly boy.*)

FIRST BOY (*looking into the wings*):   Look, there goes Salome!

GIRL: With her fire-red hair!

FIRST BOY: What does *she* want at the fair?

GIRL: To set your hearts afire, what else?

Scene 2

SALOME (*red-haired, in poor clothes, from the left*): I hear
  laughter, music . . . the dancing has started, hasn't it?
FIRST BOY (*coldly*): Possibly.
SALOME: Mind if I come along?
SECOND BOY: I don't see how we can prevent you.
FIRST BOY (*pointing at her hair*): What about that inflam-
  mable material?
SECOND BOY: The copper over there . . .
FIRST BOY: He doesn't trust you. You were seen driving
  your geese past the hayloft just before it burned down.
GIRL: He thinks you did it with your fire top.
SALOME: Why do you always pick on me? Just because I'm
  the only person in the village with red hair?
SECOND BOY: We've never had any red-thatched girls here,
  and we aim to keep it that way.
GIRL: If the good Lord had wanted red-haired people he'd
  have made some.
SALOME: He made *me*!
FIRST BOY: Well, I don't know about that. Hot colors are
  more in the department of the Devil.
SALOME: I can't help it if my hair is red.
SECOND BOY: Neither can we. See if you can find a little
  devil to dance with you.
THIRD BOY: I'll dance with her. What do I have to lose?
FIRST BOY: Oh, come on! You can do better than that!
THIRD BOY: I suppose you're right.
SECOND BOY: Let's go. Let's dance. We've wasted enough
  time! (*Off-stage music plays "Let's dance."*)
ALL: Let's go and dance!

(*All leave except Salome.*)

Scene 3

SALOME: So I'm left behind again, lonesome and blue. And why? Because my hair is red. But red is a wonderful color — the most beautiful flowers are roses, and everybody knows they are red — violets are blue. The most beautiful part of the day is the morning, and it dawns red. Even dark clouds are lovely when they're touched by the fiery red of a setting sun. Why is it that what people admire in a garden and in a sky they hate on a person's head? But what's the use? None of the fellows will take me to the dance. And if I go alone, the girls will cackle. I'd rather stay with my geese . . . they cackle at me, not about me.

(*Exits right foreground.*)

Scene 4

FLORA (*angrily*): Shame on the stagecoach. The city is within spitting distance, and yet the trip takes an hour and a half.

POPONSEED (*slow moving, carrying a large basket*): Oh! So that's why it's called a coach. It needs to be coached to run.

FLORA: Shut up and come on! You're so slow you'd make a pretty good stagecoach yourself.

POPONSEED: Oh, no, not me. I don't want to be a stagecoach — everybody's riding me enough as it is.

FLORA: I see this is one of your witty days, when you're even more unbearable than usual.

POPONSEED: Nag! Nag! Nag! You're the most naggative woman I know. Well, I'm glad it'll soon be over for me.

FLORA: Are you going to quit on me?

POPONSEED: No such luck, lady. But pretty soon you'll catch yourself a husband again . . . and then you'll have a new victim to pick on.

FLORA: I'll never marry again! I'm going to remain faithful to my late husband.

POPONSEED: Perhaps he believes that now. He never did when he was alive.

FLORA (*coquettish*):   And what if I did marry again?

POPONSEED: I wish you would! I'd even dance at your wedding. I've never found anything distasteful in seeing someone else getting married.

FLORA: Men aren't perfect but they're the best opposite sex we've got.

POPONSEED: Marriage is a gamble. Like custard pie — you never know whether it'll end up in your stomach or in your face.

FLORA: Blockhead! I don't know how I can stand you — slow and clumsy and full of foolosophy. But I've already spoken to Lady Cypressa about hiring an assistant. A strong, capable assistant, that's what I need. (*Exits through the garden gate, right.*)

POPONSEED (*alone*):   I know what's eating her. (*Winking at the audience*) It isn't the garden that needs the capable assistant!

(*Exits right.*)

Scene 5

TITUS (*entering from the right*):

SONG

You wouldn't believe what some people believe:
A piglet brings luck, a black cat makes you grieve,
A bird makes you happy, a bat makes you shiver,

If you die on a Friday, that's bad for your liver.
Some people think witches still live in this nation
And that brooms are the means of their air transportation;
But they travel by coach, drawn by one horse or two,
And coffee with schlag has replaced witch's brew.
   Superstition, superstition!
   What convenient condition!
   If a good thing or a bum thing,
   People must believe in *some*thing.

I once told a man that black cats have me scared.
The man simply shrugged and ironically stared.
He drew himself up and he said, "Oh, come on,
You know that the era of reason's begun."
I asked for a job. He would hem and would haw,
He looked at my hair, didn't like what he saw.
But he did not believe in taboos, and he said
That among his best friends there are some who are red.
   Superstition, superstition!
   What convenient condition!
   If a good thing or a bum thing,
   People must believe in *some*thing.

ENCORE

Reliance on science is always in season,
And yet we believe many things without reason.
We know we'll succeed with the opposite sex
If we just spray ourselves with deodorant X.
We think banknotes are sound if there's gold in the mint,
That something is true if we see it in print,
That no one bakes coffee cake just like our Mom,
And that problems are solved at the drop of a bomb.
   Superstition, superstition!

What convenient condition!
If a good thing or bum thing,
People must believe in *some*thing.

They say that a man's chances are dealt like a card from the
deck of destiny — if I could find the card sharp who dealt
mine I'd club him one on the head with a spade until he
cashed in his chips. On the head . . . that's my trouble. The
head. My heart's as true as a diamond but to be a redhead in
a world that's prejudiced against red hair is to have the deck
stacked against you. Prejudice is a wall against which we can
beat our heads until they're bloody, and accomplish nothing
but making them redder than they are. I have red hair — so
people think I'm sly and deceitful. I've red hair — so people
think I'm a firebug. I've red hair — so people think. . . . Oh,
prejudice! Every time I have work and make ends meet, some
little bigot moves the ends. What I need is a bit of luck, but
luck is too busy with the rich to bother about the poor. Luck
and brains seldom go together. Fate, oh fate, deal me a joker
to show me my luck has changed!

Scene 6

POPONSEED: I"ll have a beer before I water the garden —
nothing like a beer to help you with the peas. (*Seeing
Titus*) Ha, what do we have here? A foreigner — and a red
one, too?

TITUS: Fate, I believe you've dealt me my joker!

POPONSEED (*to himself*): Could this be Flora's new gardener? Strong, capable . . . yes. But the hair . . . ugh! He
looks capable of anything. (*To Titus*) Are you looking for
work?

TITUS: I'd go even that far to get a little money.

POPONSEED (*half to himself*): His hair! He's a robber!

TITUS: Not yet. My talent in that field is still undeveloped.
POPONSEED: Do you know anything about gardening?
TITUS: My qualifications lie in many directions.
POPONSEED: You must be the capable assistant the gardener's
widow is looking for.
TITUS: Assistant to a gardener's widow? A fertile field — as
I said, my qualifications lie in many directions.
POPONSEED: Not a chance! This is a gardener's widow who
doesn't like carrot tops!

(*Exits, nose-in-air, through the gate.*)

Scene 7

TITUS (*looking after Poponseed, furious*):   I'm profoundly
confounded and confoundedly dumbfounded. This bird is
so cocksure in his rudeness, he must have practiced all his
life. I was a fool to expect this place to be different — it's
peopled with people, and there's the rub! Studious research
has shown me that you must hate people before you get to
know them, and despise them afterward. Expect the worst
of people, even of yourself, and you rarely guess wrong.
Every human being spends most of his time being inhuman. I hate you, inhuman humanity. I'd become a hermit
if I could live on roots and berries. But I'm too hungry.
No, unkind mankind, you shall not lose me; appetite is
the tender bond that links me with you, and reminds me
three times a day that in spite of the color of my hair, I'm
part of the human family. Too often I've known that bitter
feeling of so much hunger that out of sheer thirst I didn't
know where to sleep the next night. (*Looking to the right*)
Good gracious, there's a reddish goldilocks guiding a
gaggle of geese through the gate. I have to take a gander.

Scene 8

(Salome enters from the right, a loaf of bread and a knife in her basket.)

SALOME: A strange young man . . . with beautiful hair!

TITUS (*to himself*):   I wonder if little radish-head will call me a carrot top, too. Maybe she has something eatable in that basket. (*Aloud*) God be with you, kindred spirit!

SALOME: I'm your servant, Sir.

TITUS (*half to himself*):   She's polite to me. That's the first person who ever . . .

SALOME: Oh, Sir, I'm the least in the town. I'm the goose-girl. I'm poor.' My name is Salome.

TITUS: Poor? I'm sorry to hear it. I'm sure you rear your young geese in the most conscientious way. Your colleagues in the big city bring up their young-lady geese, year after year, without any noble end in view. You prepare yours for the benefit of all mankind—for the banquet table.

SALOME: I can't understand you—I mean, you talk so . . . fine. You must come from a fine family. Who's your father?

TITUS: At present he is a deceased teacher.

SALOME: How nice. And your mother?

TITUS: Before her untimely demise she was for a period of time the wedded wife of her nuptial spouse.

SALOME: Ah, that's nice!

TITUS (*to himself*):   She finds everything nice — no matter what I say.

SALOME: And what's your name?

TITUS: Titus.

SALOME: That's an unusual and beautiful name. And you have no other relatives?

TITUS: Oh yes. My family tree shows distinct traces of an uncle. But he won't do a thing for me.

SALOME: Maybe he hasn't got a thing.

TITUS: He's a beer salesman, and beer is a commodity for which there is an unquenchable demand. He's foaming with money.

SALOME: Then you must have done something he didn't like.

TITUS: I have indeed. I've hit his most sensitive spot, his eye. Whenever he looks at me he sees red, and he doesn't like it.

SALOME: What? His own flesh and blood?

TITUS: The color of his blood doesn't prevent him from discriminating against my hair. And from the color of my hair he's jumped to conclusions about my character. Uncle Bung holds the world's record in conclusion jumping, and has excluded me from heart, hearth, and heritage.

SALOME: That's not nice.

TITUS: It's stupid. Nature gives us a gentle hint. What animal dislikes red? The bull — the more bull a man has in him the more violently he reacts to red.

SALOME: How clever you talk. One wouldn't know just looking at you.

TITUS: I'm not used to admiration. Uncle Bung's slap in the face was only one of many. I got it from all sides. I tried love, hoping love was color blind — but it wasn't. Friendship? A redhead has no friends, only people who'll tolerate him. Work? I was suspected of everything from theft to arson. So I've thrown off love like a topcoat, friendship like a jacket, ambition like a shirt, and here I stand, an ideological stripteaser, in the underpants of freedom.

SALOME: And you like that?

TITUS: I would, if I had an umbrella to protect me against the storms of life. It's true that the rain is falling on the rich and the poor alike, but the rich have all the umbrellas. A poor man must eat, too. When he smells food, all other passions disappear. He has no anger, no emotions, no sadness, no love, no hate, not even a soul. He has nothing but an appetite.

SALOME: I'll tell you what. My brother works in a bakery. I'll ask the baker. Maybe he needs another helper.

TITUS: My only chance to roll in dough. Did your brother bake this bread? (*Points at the bread in Salome's basket.*) Let's see how far your brother has advanced in the science of bread-making.

SALOME: Have a taste. But it's not the good kind. (*Cuts off a small piece.*)

TITUS (*eating*): Hm — let me see . . .

SALOME: My geese like it but they have no sense . . .

TITUS: The true scientist must form his own conclusions . . .

SALOME: Well, what do you say? It's not very good, is it?

TITUS: Hum. To judge your brother's work I must do more research. I need a larger sample. (*Takes the loaf and cuts off a large slice.*) I shall give you a full report in due time. (*Puts the slice in his pocket.*)

SALOME: I'll go right away and see if there's a job for you at the baker's.

TITUS: I'm counting on your brother's nepotism.

SALOME: I'll try. (*Looking left, frightened*) Oh — look!

TITUS (*looking*): Heavens — the carriage! The horse has gone wild — it's running straight to the river. (*Runs off into the left wing.*)

Scene 9

SALOME: Oh no! Be careful! Don't run right into the horse! My . . . he grabs it! (*Screaming*) Ah! The horse stands still . . . he stopped it! What a daredevil! A man gets out of the carriage . . . pale as a ghost . . . he can hardly stand up straight! Heavens, I must tell the baker about this! When he hears what Titus did, he'll give him a job for sure!

(*Exits right.*)

Scene 10

(*Titus re-enters from the left, with Monsieur Marquis.*)

MARQUIS: Ah! The fright's still in my bones!

TITUS: Will it please Your Honor to sit down and rest?

MARQUIS (*sitting down on a stone bench*):   Damned nag! It has never run away like this!

TITUS: Does it please Your Honor to feel a charley horse?

MARQUIS: No, my friend, I'm all right.

TITUS: Or perhaps a broken arm?

MARQUIS: Thank God, I'm still in one piece.

TITUS: Or a small crack in your skull?

MARQUIS: Nothing at all. I'm fine again, and all there remains to be done is to give you, as a token of my gratitude . . .

TITUS: Don't mention it.

MARQUIS: Three boys stood there, they all knew me. But all they did was shout, "Monsieur Marquis! Your carriage! It'll plunge into the water . . ."

TITUS: What? I saved a Marquis?

MARQUIS (*continuing*):   But they didn't lift a finger. Then you came . . . a swift savior . . .

TITUS (*with false modesty*):   Only doing my duty . . .

MARQUIS: Just at the crucial moment . . .

TITUS: Lucky coincidence.

MARQUIS (*standing up*):   Your modesty embarrasses me. I

don't know how I can thank you — money can never repay
what you've done . . .

Titus: Oh, money has a way of . . .

Marquis: Offending a man of your sensitivity.

Titus: Well — you see . . .

Marquis: I see your character clearly. It would cheapen
your noble deed if one would try to measure it with money.

Titus: It all depends . . .

Marquis: It depends on *who* performed the deed. It reminds me of the story of . . . his name escapes me . . . who
saved the life of Prince what's his name. Anyway, the
Prince wanted to reward our hero with diamonds, but our
hero simply said: "I find my highest reward in my conscience!" I'm sure you feel no less noble than the man
whose name I forget.

Titus: Yet, there are circumstances where a thank offering . . .

Marquis: Can be spoiled by many words. You're quite right.
True gratitude is silent. Let's not talk about the incident.

Titus (*to himself*):   The Marquis has so much tact — if he
were a cheapskate, the result would be the same.

Marquis (*looking at Titus' hair*):   But, friend, I've just noticed something — hum, hum! This head of yours — it must
be an embarrassment to you!

Titus: It is indeed. But it's the only head I have, I can't buy
myself another one.

Marquis: Well, perhaps . . . let me . . . a small souvenir you
must accept. I insist! Just wait here a moment!

(*Exits left.*)

Scene 11

Titus: One more minute, and he'd have called me, out of
gratitude, a red beet. A fine Marquis I picked to save!

(*Looking to the left*) Look at him run to his carriage! Well, he does rummage around — maybe he'll give me a present after all. A souvenir, he said. Now he's picked up something — for heaven's sakes, a hat box! Is he going to give me an old hat for saving his young life?

Scene 12

MARQUIS (*with a hat box*):   Here, friend, take this, and make good use of it. It will be a talisman for you (*Gives him the box*) and I would be pleased if I'd be the architect of your good fortune. Goodbye, friend, and God bless you!

(*Exits left.*)

Scene 13

TITUS (*alone, box in hand*):   Architect of my fortune? Talisman? Now I'm really curious about what's in here. (*Opens the box and pulls out a black wig.*) A wig! Nothing but a pitch-coal-black wig! (*Calling after Marquis*) I'll teach you to make fun of me, you pompous penny-pincher! But — wait a minute: didn't I always want a wig to hide my red top? Hasn't it been just those lousy fifty thalers that stood between me and being one of them? Talisman, he said — he's right! I'll put on this wig, and I'll be accepted for what I really am, and not for what shows on top of my head. What do I have to lose? I'll try it! The world will open up for me, just like this gate! (*Opens the gate.*)

Scene 14

SALOME (*from the right*):   Oh, Mr. Titus, I've bad news!
TITUS (*turning to Salome*):   What it it?

SALOME: The baker won't take you. When he heard about . . . (*Points to his head.*)

TITUS: Oh, it doesn't matter — I'm going to the mansion to find work.

SALOME: The mansion? Oh, don't even try. If Lady Cypressa sees you she'll chase you out. (*Referring to her hair*) I must never be seen in the mansion.

TITUS: The prejudices of the Lady are of no concern to me. From now on, the most important thing is what I have in here (*Pointing at his temple*) and not out there! (*Points at his hair.*)

SALOME: Well, I wish you luck. I know I shouldn't feel that way but it still hurts that another hope has dropped down the well.

TITUS: What hope?

SALOME: That you might stay. People would have said, "These two are the homeliest couple in the village. The red Titus, and the red Salome." No other girl would have looked at you, just as no other boy looks at me.

TITUS: We would have had a mutual monopoly on each other's homeliness!

SALOME: We might have become friends.

TITUS: And from friendship to love is only one happy step.

SALOME: I haven't dared to think that far.

TITUS: Why not? Thoughts are free.

SALOME: I don't know — for some you pay with sleepless nights.

TITUS: You have to take your chances. Man proposes . . . (*To himself*) the wig disposes, in my case. (*Aloud*) Well, adieu, Salome.

SALOME: Don't be so proud, Mr. Titus. Take my hand, like a friend, and say, "See you later, Salome."

TITUS: You are right. (*Takes her hand.*)We part as friends. See you later.

SALOME: Yes, and I *will* see you later.

TITUS: You might.

SALOME: Oh yes. You go through that gate, and through the same gate they'll throw you out. (*Points at the bench.*) And I'll sit here . . .

TITUS: And wait until someone will boot me into your arms. Well, I am accepting my fate, whatever it is.

SALOME: Are you going in there, to work and get rich?

TITUS: Let's not confuse the issue. Hard and honest work is good enough to make a living. To get rich you must use a different approach.

(*Exits through the gate.*)

Scene 15

SALOME (*alone*):   There he goes — and I'm left high and dry. And yet I feel so low and my eyes are wet. I never had much luck, and now it feels as if he'd taken even the little I had with him. All a girl can do is sit and wait. A man can at least go out and kick. Yes, it's a man's world.

SONG

When a girl is in love with a man who is not —
Well, what can she do? Not a heck of a lot.
She can cry, she can moan, she can hang herself, drown . . .
But look what goes on if a man is turned down:
He goes to the tavern and orders a beer,
And flirts with the waitress and whoever is near,
And he may not slow down till the field he has played —
    Yes, a man has it made, has it made, has it made!

When a girl has her first or her second affair,
Her reputation is ruined beyond all repair.

But a man with a harem of ten or a score
Will still attract girls, and the merrier the more.
In fact, they would probably fall for him good,
And if not from love, then from envy they would.
His reputation gets better with each escapade —
    Yes, a man has it made, has it made, has it made!

A woman is always a slave to her fashion,
She has to fake nature to rouse a man's passion.
With girdles and cheaters she must prove her sex:
Where she is concave she must look like convex.
And her hair — she must curl it, and braid it, and tint it,
And if she's in love, she may only just hint it.
But a man needs no girdle, no curl, and no braid —
    Yes, a man has it made, has it made, has it made!

Encore

The twentieth century brought on a sequel:
The woman has gained her position as equal.
Women vote, run for office, and dress up in trousers,
Become independent, divorce their dear spousers,
Or go to a school where they pick up some knowledge.
But they then take a job, put their husbands through college,
Run to work, run the house, overworked, underpaid —
    Yes, men *still* have it made, have it made, have it made!

Scene 16

(*A room in the apartment of Flora, the chief gardener. Door in the middle and right, window left.*)

FLORA: Trouble and headaches! The pickles I get into grow
like weeds — I can't get rid of them all by myself. My dear

husband, God bless his soul, told me to stay a widow and carry on as a chief gardener — how can a blessed soul have such a wretched idea? The helpers have no respect, they pay no attention, they need a man. And why fool myself — I need a man, too. Will my husband forgive me? Sometimes I can't believe that the dead watch us from the Beyond. How can they be in a state of bliss if they see what's going on down here? I can see my dear departed shake his head in the clouds. What if he decides to appear one night — as a ghost? What if he comes down and knocks at my door? (*There is a knock at the door. She screams.*) Aaah! (*Supports herself on the table.*)

Scene 17

Titus (*in black wig; enters at center stage*): Sorry, lady, but do you always scream "Aaah!" instead of saying "Come in"?
Flora (*collecting herself*): I got scared.
Titus (*to himself*): Strange — she's afraid when someone knocks. Most women of her age are afraid that no one will knock.
Flora: You're probably surprised that my nerves are so weak?
Titus: Surprised about the normal? Nerves made of spiderwebs, hearts of wax, and heads of steel — that's the structure of the female anatomy.
Flora (*to herself*): The man has charm . . . and the romantic dark hair . . . (*Aloud*) What can I do for you?
Titus: You can do a great deal for me. I'm for hire.
Flora: Are you a gardener?
Titus: Of sorts. I've sown prejudice, I've planted suspicion — and you should have seen how they took root and grew!
Flora: Very clever, but . . .

TITUS: Now I'm ready to experiment with a new crop —
love. The heart is said to be a fertile ground, if you cultivate
it right . . .

FLORA: I must say you have a fresh approach to job hunting.
(*Looks at him admiringly.*) What's your background in
gardening?

TITUS: I'm an exotic plant, not native to these regions, up-
rooted by circumstances beyond my control, and now trans-
planted by fate into the flowerpot of your care, hoping to
find nourishment from the sunlight of your protection.

FLORA: Your talk is flowery enough, but what do you know
about plants?

TITUS: I know something about people, and that makes me
an expert on plants.

FLORA: I don't see how that follows.

TITUS: Oh, but it does! Most people are like plants — they
vegetate. A person who gets up day after day at the same
time, clings to his office desk until he retires climbing up in
slow promotion — he's an ivy, he vegetates; a person who
meekly opens his store every morning, politely sells his
wares to all comers, has no other recreation than his Friday
night card game — he's a mashed potato, he vegetates; a
person who comes joylessly home from his work bristling at
his wife, has nothing but barbed answers to questions from
his children, offends everyone with stinging remarks — he's
a cactus, he vegetates; and a person who is so thin-skinned
that he makes everyone cry who comes near him — he's an
onion, he vegetates. Even the highest form of human life,
the millionaire, is really only lettuce turned into man.

FLORA: You must have studied the higher fields of horticul-
ture. Your head seems as bright inside as it is black outside.

TITUS: Don't you like my hair?

FLORA (*coquettish*): You know very well how handsome
dark locks look on a man!

TITUS: It's news to *me*!

FLORA: You really want a job here? All right, you're hired. But not as a helper. You have brains, manners, looks . . . (*Titus bows.*)

FLORA: You'll work directly under me. I'll make you gardener to supervise the helpers.

TITUS: I don't know how to thank you.

FLORA: We'll find a way. (*Looking at his hair*) I've never seen such coal-black raven hair! Are you Italian?

TITUS: My mother was a gardener from Sicily. She was no wallflower — a real bachelor's button.

FLORA: You silly man. And how vain you are! I believe you curl your hair. (*Wants to touch his hair.*)

TITUS (*drawing back*): Don't touch. My head is a very ticklish problem.

FLORA (*dreamily*): My husband was very ticklish, too. (*Back to reality*) But what really is ticklish is how to present you to Lady Cypressa. You can't show yourself in this outfit!

TITUS: I don't see why a gardener shouldn't be wearing a seedy suit . . .

FLORA: Go into the next room. In the big chest you'll find the suits and shoes of my beloved husband. Try them on — I think they'll be your size.

TITUS: The suits of your beloved . . . ? And I'll be in his shoes? (*Touches his locks coquettishly.*) How can I help it if certain feelings begin to sprout . . . (*Looks at her significantly and exits right.*)

Scene 18

FLORA: A charming man! Well, you never know — I might catch myself a second husband before Madam Constantia catches hers! She acts so high and mighty because she's the Lady's maid and has a lover. A lover, yes, but I bet that barber of hers hasn't said a word about marriage! I have a feeling that I'll be able to get my handsome blacktop to chase me where I want him. Right up the aisle. (*Sighing*) To catch a husband is the perfect end of a marry chase. But now I'll have to tell the rest of my crew. (*Calls through the window*) Poponseed, come here!

(*Poponseed comes in slowly.*)

FLORA: Call all the helpers together and tell them I've hired a gardener. Now he'll do the bossing, not I.

POPONSEED: Aye, aye. *Anything* will be an improvement. (*Exits.*)

FLORA: Don't be fresh! (*Looking through the window*) Oh-oh! The Lady's maid? Coming here? That means trouble.

Scene 19

CONSTANTIA (*enters center stage*):   Flora . . .

FLORA (*with a curtsy*):   At your service.

CONSTANTIA: My Lady is not satisfied with the care of the garden.

FLORA: It's not my fault. The help . . . but it will be different from now on. I've hired a most promising gardener.

CONSTANTIA: Good. I'll inform the Lady.

FLORA: I'd like to take the liberty of presenting him myself.

CONSTANTIA: Are you out of your mind? Present a country clod to the Lady?

FLORA: Oh, I beg your pardon. He's not an ordinary gardener, he's a most unusual . . .

Scene 20

(Titus enters in an old-fashioned gardener's suit, from the right, holding a bundle. He speaks to Flora without noticing Constantia.)

TITUS: Well, here I am. Does this suit bring back sweet memories?

CONSTANTIA *(to herself)*: What a magnificent mop of hair!

TITUS: I've bundled up my own things.

FLORA: Just put them there! *(Points at a chair, left.)*

TITUS: All right. *(Turns as he sees Constantia.)* Ah! You couldn't draw a drop of blood even if you'd stick a pin in me! *(Bowing before Constantia)* I beg of you . . . *(To Flora)* Why didn't you tell me . . . ? *(To Constantia, with a deep bow)* . . . not to be angry with me if I . . . *(To Flora)* . . . that Her Ladyship is present . . . *(To Constantia, with a deep bow)* . . . didn't pay my respects right away . . . *(To Flora)* . . . It really is awful — in what a situation you put me!

CONSTANTIA: I'm not Her Ladyship.

FLORA: What gave you that idea?

TITUS: Your Ladyship just wants to spare my feelings . . .

FLORA: This is Constantia, the Lady's maid.

TITUS: No, I don't believe it! The noble forehead, the imperial glimmer of the eyes, the aristocratic curve of the elbow!

CONSTANTIA *(flattered)*: I assure you I'm only the Lady's maid.

TITUS: Really? I only believe it because I hear it from your own lips. A Lady's maid? My mother was a Lady's maid, too.

FLORA: But you said your mother was a gardener.

Titus: She started out as a gardener, yes, but then she advanced to the position of Lady's maid.

Constantia (*to Flora*): Really, an interesting, well-bred man!

Flora (*to Titus, who keeps looking at Constantia*): Just put your things there.

Titus (*looking at Constantia*): What a waste to make a Lady's maid out of genuine Lady material!

Flora: Don't you hear? Put your bundle on that chair!

Titus: Yes, right away. (*Walks to the chair next to the door, still looking admiringly at Constantia.*)

Flora (*mumbling*): How she throws herself at him, that slut!

Scene 21

Poponseed (*entering, center stage*): The gardeners will be here right away.

Titus (*seeing Poponseed, turns about; to himself*): Damn it! If he recognizes me . . . (*Turns toward Constantia, with back to Poponseed.*)

Poponseed (*to Flora*): So that's the new gardener? I'd like to introduce myself. (*Steps between Titus and Constantia.*)

Titus (*turns to Flora, to have his back to Poponseed again*): Send him away. I'm no friend of ceremonies.

Flora: Oh, don't put on an act.

Poponseed (*trying to face Titus*): Mr. Gardener, meet the hardest working man in your crew . . .

Titus (*embarrassed*): That sudden draft . . . I have to . . . (*He reaches into his pocket for a handkerchief but pulls out a gray wig with a tail which he quickly holds before his face.*)

Poponseed: That's a funny handkerchief you have!

Titus: What's that?

FLORA (*laughing*):   That's the wig of my former husband.

TITUS: How former can a wig get? This one still has a tail! (*Stuffs the wig into the bundle he holds.*)

POPONSEED: What the devil! The gardener's face looks familiar. (*To Titus*) Don't you have a brother with red hair?

CONSTANTIA: How dare you!

TITUS: I have no brother at all.

POPONSEED: Well, I guess it must have been the brother of someone else.

FLORA: What do you mean, dumbbell?

POPONSEED: Oh, nothing. I just saw someone with red hair. No harm done.

Scene 22

(*Two garden helpers enter through the center stage, carrying baskets with fruit.*)

HELPER: Here's the fruit for the Lady.

FLORA: Take it up to the mansion.

CONSTANTIA: That's not the way, to have the servants take up the fruit.

FLORA: That's the way we've always done it.

CONSTANTIA: The new gardener will present the fruit, and that's also a suitable occasion to present *him*.

FLORA: Present him? How so? You just told me we can't present a country clod to the Lady.

CONSTANTIA (*embarrassed*):   Yes, but — that is . . .

TITUS: Country clod?

FLORA (*enjoying Constantia's embarrassment*):   That's what she said!

TITUS: Country clod!

CONSTANTIA (*very embarrassed*): I have . . .

TITUS: That's terrible!

FLORA: You're so right! It's . . .

TITUS: . . . a mystery to me (*To Flora*) how you can think the words "country clod" refer to me.

FLORA: These were Madame Constantia's words.

TITUS (*to Flora*): Let me tell you, there are plenty of country clods around. I'm not such an egoist that I would claim the words only for myself.

CONSTANTIA (*recovering*): I just meant . . .

TITUS (*pointing at Constantia*): If Madame really brought such words over her beautiful lips, she must have meant one of the helpers. (*Pointing at the servants*) She hadn't met me yet, so how could she appraise my cloddishness? (*To Constantia*) Am I not right?

CONSTANTIA: Absolutely.

FLORA (*very angry*): You want to call me a liar?

TITUS: No. Merely a slanderer.

CONSTANTIA (*to Titus*): You come with me now.

FLORA: What's the rush? The Lady isn't home yet.

CONSTANTIA: That's why. I — uh — mean it's more appropriate for the gardener to wait for her, than for her to wait for him.

TITUS: That's obvious. (*To Constantia, referring to Flora*) She knows nothing of etiquette. The most proper place to wait for Her Ladyship is with the Lady's maid.

FLORA (*to herself*): I could tear her to pieces, the bitch!

TITUS: And it's also proper that I present myself, as a garden supervisor, in a manner that — ah, here we are! (*Goes to the window and pulls flowers from the flowerpots.*)

FLORA: My flowers!

TITUS: Just the thing for a bouquet. Now for a ribbon . . . (*Takes a wide satin ribbon from the table and wraps it around the flowers.*)

FLORA: Heavens! The new satin ribbon I bought for my evening gown!

TITUS: For such an occasion the best is barely good enough. (*To Constantia, pointing at Flora*) She knows nothing of etiquette.

Scene 23

(*Several helpers enter at center stage.*)

HELPERS: We came to welcome the new gardener!

TITUS: Greetings, my good fellows. You're just in time. Come on, carry the baskets.

HELPERS: Yes, Sir.

CONSTANTIA (*to Titus*): This is the occasion to establish your place and earn the loyalty of your crew. The best way to do it is to circulate a little money. At least that's what I've found . . .

TITUS: I've found that, too, Madame, but (*Fingering his vest pocket*) . . . what I don't find . . .

CONSTANTIA: Oh, it will be my pleasure . . . (*Wants to give him a purse.*)

FLORA: Excuse me, that's my business. Here. (*Wants to give him a purse.*)

CONSTANTIA (*preventing it*): No, this won't do. It's a matter of honor for the house, and the Lady will want me to handle it.

FLORA: I'll put it on the Lady's bill. It's up to me as chief gardener . . .

TITUS: Excuse me, ladies, but this matter can easily be disposed of without any hurt feelings. I'll take the liberty . . . (*Takes the purse from Constantia.*) Just hand it over . . . (*Takes the money from Flora.*) There! Avoid all friction, that's my motto. (*To the helpers*) I'll treat you all!

HELPERS: Hooray!
TITUS: And now, on to the mansion!

(Exits with Constantia, followed by the helpers carrying the baskets. Flora glares after them, and Poponseed watches her with amusement. The helpers cheer.)

CURTAIN

ACT TWO

(Lady Cypressa's garden. In the right foreground the gardener's cottage of Flora, with entrance. Table and garden chairs. In the background a wing of the mansion.)

Scene 1

(Poponseed and several helpers are sitting around the table, drinking.)

HELPERS: Come on! Another round of wine!

POPONSEED: That's right. We still have half the money left, it must be spent on drinks! We can't quit now.

HELPER: "Don't quit now" — that's what Flora always says.

POPONSEED: Just remember, a gardener is a plant that's always thirsty. It must be wetted!

HELPER: But not with water!

(All laugh and drink.)

HELPERS: Hooray for the new supervisor! A generous man! Hooray for the new gardener!

POPONSEED: Horsemanure! He's a lazy lout, I know the type. He'll put his hands in his pockets, his feet on the table, and will make us work, work, work!

125

HELPERS: Well in that case we'll . . .
POPONSEED: Not now. Let's not spoil our party. Later, when
we're back at work we can take time out to fret about him.
Everything at the proper time!

Scene 2

FLORA (*with a basket, from the house*): Now be off with
your glasses. I need the table.
HELPERS: We were about to quit anyway.
POPONSEED: It's a party in honor of your gardener.
FLORA (*to helpers*): Go back to work!
HELPERS (*leaving*): All right, we're going.

(*Helpers leave.*)

Scene 3

POPONSEED: I don't see how you can have the heart to break
up a garden party.
FLORA (*has taken a tablecloth from the basket and spreads
it over the table*): Shut up and help me set the table for
dinner.
POPONSEED: Aye, aye, you don't have to order me twice to
do *that* job. (*Takes plates and silver from the basket.*) Only
for two?
FLORA: A dinner for two.
POPONSEED: Does the new gardener take his meal in the
mansion, with the Lady's maid?
FLORA: Dummkopf. He'll eat here with me.
POPONSEED: Now, let's see — he, you, and me — that makes
three.
FLORA: I've let you eat here in the past because I didn't

want to sit all by myself. Now I have the gardener to keep
me company. You will disappear when the meal is served.

POPONSEED (*annoyed*): That was one time I *never* disappeared.

FLORA: Don't argue and bring the soup.

POPONSEED: Now? It'll get cold. God knows when he'll show
up.

FLORA (*looking impatiently toward the mansion*): He'll be
here any moment. I don't understand what's keeping him.

POPONSEED: I'm beginning to understand.

FLORA: Hush, and do as you're told.

POPONSEED: The capable assistant must be busy in the mansion, taking care of tu-lips — that's what's keeping him.

(*Exits into the gardener's cottage.*)

Scene 4

FLORA (*alone*): That's the last time I'll let him go up there!
The way Constantia digs her hooks into him, it's disgusting!

TITUS (*from the mansion, napkin tied around his neck, a
chicken leg in his hand*): Ah, you there, good to see you . . .

FLORA: Upon my word, what's keeping you? The dinner's
waiting.

TITUS: I'm not. I've been waited on.

FLORA: At the mansion?

TITUS: In the Lady's maid's chamber. Dined and wined. Look
at this chicken — that's the last leg of his journey on earth.

FLORA: It's quite improper for you to sponge off Constantia.
I won't hear of it! (*Snaps her fingers.*)

TITUS: You're damn right, you won't hear of it: On account
of it's none of your business. I'm no longer under your
green thumb, I have slipped through your fingers, you snap-
dragon. I've accepted a better position.

FLORA: What?

TITUS: But I do owe you something, so wait a moment. I'll be back. (*Withdraws into the house.*)

FLORA (*alone*): Constantia, this is your work! A widow with a lover of her own who snatches someone else's beau — in my book that's a human spittoon!

Scene 5

POPONSEED (*carrying a pot*): Here's the soup.

TITUS (*coming back*): And here's the suit. The late lamented gardener's garb. Compliments of the new management! (*Tosses the bundle at Poponseed and withdraws.*)

POPONSEED: Missed me! What is it?

FLORA (*to Poponseed*): Oh, go jump in the lake!

POPONSEED: Won't you eat?

FLORA: No! If you don't lose your appetite over this, then you've got no appetite to lose!

POPONSEED: Well, I thought this was to be the cozy dinner for two where I wasn't wanted.

FLORA: Go to hell! (*Exits.*)

POPONSEED (*alone*): What do you know! He doesn't dine here, she doesn't dine here, and I — who was sent packing — I dine for the two of them. Oh Fate, shrouded in mystery, you surprise me with such an unexpected fit of justice! (*Sits down; eats the soup.*)

Scene 6

(*Room in the mansion. Center and two side doors. Titus enters in an elegant gamekeeper's uniform.*)

Titus (*alone*): History repeats itself in a hurry: one widow acts like the other, offers me the defunct clothes of the departed husband. Now this one wants me to be Lady Cypressa's gamekeeper. Well, if that means nothing more than opening the carriage door and hopping onto the running board — that's as much of gamekeeping as I know. Oh, wig, you have done wonders — the food is delicious, the wine exquisite. I really don't know whether it's my changing luck or the Tokay that's gone to my head.

Scene 7

Constantia (*entering*): Ah, that's the way to be dressed! Your countenance is much better suited to a gamekeeper's uniform than to a gardener's outfit.

Titus: I hope Madame will share your views about my countenance. Or in the end I'll be back with shovel and spade.

Constantia: You don't have much confidence in my influence around here, do you? My late husband was the gamekeeper, and the Lady certainly won't expect me to remain a widow forever.

Titus: Such divine features must not be condemned to widowhood for life.

Constantia: Suppose I'd marry again. Do you doubt that Lady Cypressa would give my husband a position in the mansion?

Titus: Any such doubt would be blasphemy.

Constantia: I don't say this because I have designs on you . . .

Titus: Of course not. You're entirely undesigned.

Constantia: My interest in a gamekeeper is strictly professional.

Titus: I realize that. I'm game.

CONSTANTIA: I'm not the kind of animal that shops around for a husband, but I do need a man trained in animal husbandry.

TITUS: I get the difference.

CONSTANTIA: I only mention it to show you that I do carry weight around here . . .

TITUS (*ogling her*): You do carry quite a little. Around here.

CONSTANTIA: . . . and can get a man in the position I want him in when I throw that weight around.

TITUS (*to himself*): Oh raven-black skull, you're performing red-letter-day miracles!

CONSTANTIA: My husband, God bless him . . .

TITUS: God blessed him at the time He placed him in your arms, not now, when the poor wretch has to look down on his divine widow from a mere heaven. Oh, Constantia, one pays marriage a poor compliment by calling only those husbands "blessed" who have departed!

CONSTANTIA: So you think that one could, at my side . . .

TITUS: . . . walk on clouds and look into all sorts of heavens!

CONSTANTIA: Flatterer!

TITUS (*to himself*): Metaphysics is a good place to dip for applesauce. (*Aloud*) I think I hear voices.

Scene 8

SALOME (*shyly entering through the middle*): Excuse me . . .

TITUS (*scared, to himself*): What the devil — Salome! (*Throws himself nonchalantly into a chair, so she can't see his face.*)

CONSTANTIA: How did you get in here?

SALOME: There was no one outside, so I thought it was the entry to the hall . . . I never realized . . . please, Madame, come outside with me . . . I can't even talk properly standing in the midst of such luxury . . .

CONSTANTIA: Stop fussing. What do you want?

SALOME: I'm looking for someone I've already looked for at the gardener's — but he wasn't there, so I came here.

CONSTANTIA (*suspiciously*): *Whom* are you looking for?

SALOME: For a man with red hair.

CONSTANTIA (*relieved*): Well, you'll easily find *him*. He'll glow in the dark. (*Titus winces.*)

CONSTANTIA: You won't find him here, that is certain. I would not tolerate such a being — nor would my Lady — we share a justifiable prejudice against both scarlet men and scarlet women.

SALOME: Well, if you happen to run into him, tell him that there are people from the city here who've asked me all sorts of funny questions about him . . .

TITUS (*forgetting himself, turning*): And what did you tell them?

SALOME (*frightened*): What's that? (*Recognizes Titus.*) Ah! (*She faints in Constantia's arms.*)

CONSTANTIA: What's the matter with her? (*To Titus*) Go on, bring a chair, I can't hold her forever.

TITUS (*bringing a chair*): There. Set her down.

CONSTANTIA (*sets her down*): Look at her. She doesn't move. (*To Titus*) That's strange. She fainted when she saw you.

TITUS (*embarrassed*): I'm not that much of a knockout.

CONSTANTIA: But you see she doesn't move.

TITUS (*very embarrassed*): Yes, I see that.

CONSTANTIA: Now . . . it seems . . . yes, she moved!

TITUS: Yes, I see that, too. I'll go and get her a glass of water. (*Wants to leave.*)

CONSTANTIA: You stay. Or do you have reasons to sneak off?

TITUS: Why should I? I don't know the person.

CONSTANTIA: Then you need not be afraid that she'd wake up.

SALOME (*recuperating*): Oh, Madame . . . I'm beginning to feel better . . .

CONSTANTIA: What's the matter with you?

SALOME: This man . . .

CONSTANTIA: So you know him?

SALOME: No, oh no, I don't. I don't know him at all. (*Getting up*) It's just . . . when he so suddenly spoke to me . . .

CONSTANTIA: Is that why you fainted?

SALOME: It's silly, isn't it . . . city nerves in a country girl! (*To Titus, who watches her in amazement*) Don't be angry with me, Sir, and if you happen to see the one with the red hair tell him I meant well, I just wanted to warn him. I certainly won't tell anything to the people who're asking about him. Tell him I surely won't stand in his way if he wants to make his fortune . . . (*Suppressing her tears*) Tell him that, if you happen to see the one with the red hair. (*To Constantia*) And again, forgive me for fainting in rooms that are out of my class, and God bless you, both of you, and . . . (*Breaking into tears*) now I'm beginning to cry . . . that's not proper . . . please forgive me, I'm such a silly goose.

(*Hurries out the middle, crying.*)

Scene 9

CONSTANTIA (looking after her, surprised): I daresay, I find the whole episode highly suspicious.

TITUS (*recovering*): Why?

CONSTANTIA: She was so moved, so stirred up . . .

TITUS: About someone with red hair. She said so.

CONSTANTIA: She spoke of him, yes, but it was you who seemed to affect her.

TITUS: Now how can I affect her?

CONSTANTIA: You can't deny that she was moved.

TITUS: That's not my fault. First you blame me that she didn't move, then that she was moved. I really don't know —

CONSTANTIA: Now don't be angry. I may be wrong to connect you with such a common person — it would be unbelievable!

TITUS: It would indeed. I'm a man set on his career. (*Crudely hinting*) My romantic ideas float in regions high above the riffraff.

CONSTANTIA (*coquettishly*): Oh? Well, it was lucky that the Lady wasn't present at that disgusting scene. She hates the common. Her interests are intellectual — just as mine. She is an author.

TITUS: An author? She writes?

CONSTANTIA: Poetry. We have many literary teas in the mansion — you know something about literature, don't you?

TITUS: I know more about tea, but it doesn't matter. I know all about writers. If she'll read her stuff to me and I tell her that I find it divine, she'll say, "Ah, this man has judgment . . . insight . . . a fine education!"

CONSTANTIA: You're a fox! (*To herself*) Quite a different caliber of man from my hairdresser!

Scene 10

MARQUIS (*entering through the center*): My darling Constantia . . .

TITUS (*to himself*): What the devil! My illustrious wig donor! If he talks, my career is wrecked before it started! (*Retires to the side of the stage.*)

MARQUIS: I almost missed this happy opportunity to press your lovely hand to my lips. (*Kisses her hand.*)

TITUS (*to himself*):   A marquis kissing the hand of a Lady's maid? Is that broadmindedness or dirtymindedness?

CONSTANTIA: It's so late — I didn't think you'd show up today.

MARQUIS: Believe me, only an extraordinary emergency could have prevented me — who's this? (*Notices Titus, who quickly grabs a piece of cloth from a chair and begins to dust the furniture busily.*) A new gamekeeper?

CONSTANTIA: Hired today. A man of many talents.

MARQUIS: How can you judge the talents of a gamekeeper? And anyway, what is the Lady's game that needs a keeper?

CONSTANTIA: You see how he keeps busy.

MARQUIS (*trying unsuccessfully to examine Titus' face*): Yes, but what's his game?

CONSTANTIA (*to Marquis*):   You haven't told me what happened to you.

MARQUIS (*with occasional glances at Titus*):   Oh yes. I was in a double accident: I might have drowned or broken my neck — if by a stroke of good luck a brave young man had not checked my horse . . .

CONSTANTIA: I never trusted that horse with its red mane! (*Titus winces.*)

MARQUIS: I shall believe your judgment forever, my wise Constantia. This young man then . . . (*Looking sharply at Titus*) my savior (*Turning Titus around*) I was not mistaken — it's him!

TITUS (*bowing deeply*):   Monsieur . . . please . . . you mistake me for someone else . . . (*Wants to leave.*)

MARQUIS (*holding him back*):   Why deny it, my brave man? It's you — the figure, the voice, and — humph — the color of your hair . . .

TITUS: The color of my hair has nothing to do with it.

MARQUIS: Yes, it has.

CONSTANTIA: That's right. Once you have seen these locks you don't easily forget them. A remarkable head of hair!

MARQUIS (*flattered*): Oh, thank you.

CONSTANTIA (*laughing*): You act as if you'd made it yourself. But you do know something about hair — have you ever seen such brilliance, such miraculous growth? (*Points at Titus' head as if she wanted to touch it.*)

TITUS (*drawing back*): Don't touch! It's my sensitive spot.

MARQUIS (*softly to Constantia, irritated*): You seem to take a special interest in the new servant . . .

CONSTANTIA (*a little embarrassed*): Oh, a little encouragement for the newcomer . . .

MARQUIS (*as above*): . . . which, in my opinion, is out of place in the relationship between a Lady's maid and a fellow domestic.

CONSTANTIA (*softly but sharply*): Thanks for the lesson, but I can very well judge what is and isn't out of place between me and my "fellow domestic."

MARQUIS (*to Constantia in conciliatory tone*): My dear Constantia, I merely wanted . . .

CONSTANTIA: You wanted to comb the blond page wig that the Lady is going to wear at the masquerade. You'll find it on the table in the next room. Go and do your work!

TITUS (*to Marquis*): What? You are a hairdresser? I thought you were a marquis — a cross between a baron and a duke.

MARQUIS: Marquis is my name, and I'm a wigmaker.

TITUS: Well, that's a wig of a different color! The abyss between us is quickly filling up with combs and scissors, and we can be friends. (*Offers him a hand.*)

MARQUIS (*taking his hand*): I owe you thanks . . . (*Softly*) but you owe me something, too, and don't forget it!

TITUS: I never forget a kind deed — if I did it.

CONSTANTIA: Madame will be back soon. I'll go and lay out her clothes for the evening. (*Exits center.*)

TITUS (*calling after her*): So long, charming layer outer of clothes!

Scene 11

MARQUIS: My good man, that was uncalled for . . . Constantia is my fiancée and I won't stand for such familiarities.

TITUS: Are you threatening me?

MARQUIS: I'm warning you. Don't forget your fate hangs on a hair — on a pretty bunch of dark hair.

TITUS: Could you be ungrateful enough to reveal our secret?

MARQUIS: I might be smart enough to get rid of a competitor that way.

TITUS: May I remind you that, without my intervention, you would not be the lucky fiancé of an affectionate woman but the unfortunate victim of some frigid water nymph?

MARQUIS: I owe you thanks but not an option on my bride.

TITUS: I'm not in the market for brides. I'm being pleasant to the Lady's maid not to win her heart but her patronage.

MARQUIS: Now, that's better. In that case you can count on my cooperation and, what's more, on my keeping my mouth shut. But keep your hands off my girl — or else! Just remember, your head is in my hands!

(Exits right.)

Scene 12

TITUS *(alone)*: My poor head! So much has come over it today, and into it, too. The Tokay went to my head, and that this wigmaker is Constantia's fiancé also goes around *(Pointing at his head)* in here. *(Throws himself into an easy chair.)* It's really a matter of the heart but all the heart does is flutter and dump problems into the lap of the head even if the head is up to its neck in trouble. I'm done in. *(Yawns.)* It'll be a while until Lady Cypressa comes home

. . . (*His head drops*) meanwhile . . . I could . . . (*Yawning*)
rest . . . a little . . . not fall asleep . . . just . . . rest . . . a
. . . little . . . (*Falls asleep.*)

Scene 13

MARQUIS (*coming back after a short while*):   It's too dark in
there to work on the wig — I have to find a light . . . maybe
the gamekeeper can help me. Where did he go? Has he
sneaked off to my Constantia? Now just you wait till I . . .
(*Wants to run out the center door, sees Titus in the easy
chair.*) Oh, there he is, resting like a baby . . . my silly jeal-
ousy! That's not the way a man sleeps who's madly in
love . . .
TITUS (*stammering in his sleep*):   Con — stan — stan — tia!
MARQUIS: What was that? (*Steps carefully closer.*)
TITUS (*in sleep*):   Lovely figure — Con — Con — Constantia.
MARQUIS: The louse dares dream of her!
TITUS (*in sleep*):   One — more — ki — ki — kiss!
MARQUIS: Hell's peckerneck, I don't allow such dreams! (*Is
about to grab Titus, then reconsiders*)   Wait — I have a
better idea! We'll see if she'll give a ki-ki-kiss to a red mop!
(*Cautiously takes off Titus' wig.*)
TITUS (*still asleep*):   Don't Stan — stantia . . . I'm ticklish on
. . . my head . . .
MARQUIS: Now try your luck, you red Casanova! Your talis-
man is gone forever! (*Puts wig in his pocket and exits
through center.*)

Scene 14

TITUS (*talking in his sleep*):   Ah — your — tender — hands —
(*Noise of a carriage outside, then the sharp sound of a door-*

bell. Titus wakes up.) What was that? I must have . . .
(*Runs to the center door.*) A servant is running out . . . the
Lady is coming home . . . this is *it!* Now I'm going to be
presented. (*Straightens his uniform.*) My uniform is all
crumpled . . . my tie slipped . . . I need a mirror . . . (*Runs
to a mirror at left, looks at himself, startled.*) For God's
sake, my wig's gone! It must have dropped off while I had
dropped off. (*Runs to the easy chair, looks around.*) No, it's
gone, lost, stolen! Who could be so mean as to . . . oh, of
course, the jealous pomade peddler, the sneaky hair curler,
the oily Othello. He has stolen my talisman! Now, at this
decisive, this most promising moment, I stand here, a flick-
ering candle at the coffin of my young career! But wait —
he's in there, working on the Lady's hair piece . . . he won't
get away! You'll give me back my wig, dandruff chaser, or
I'll shake your brilliantined slick soul out of your body!

(*Exits right.*)

Scene 15

CYPRESSA: I must say I find it rather impertinent of Constantia to hire a new servant without my permission.

EMMA: Don't be mad at her, Mama, I've always wanted a
gamekeeper. He will be so much more fun to have around
than our two wobbly-kneed servants in their old-fashioned
uniforms.

CYPRESSA: We don't really need a gamekeeper . . .

EMMA: But Constantia says he's such a militant-looking
black-top. He has no moustache, she says, but you must
order him to grow one. And I want him to grow whiskers,
too, black and all over his face so you can't see anything
but two blazing black eyes. Oooh! He will look magnificent
standing on the back of our carriage!

Cypressa: I'll send the man away again, and that'll be the end of it. Where is he, anyway? Titus is his name, she said. I say, Titus — Titus!

Scene 16

Titus (*in a blond wig, from the right*): Here I am, Your Ladyship, paying my humblest respects to the illustrious Lady I am to serve.

Emma (*to her mother*): What's that? That's no blacktop!

Cypressa (*to Emma*): But he has manners, the blondie.

Titus (*to himself*): Blondie? Did she say blondie?

Cypressa (*to Titus*): My maid hired you without my permission — however . . . (*To Emma*) Emma!

Titus (*to himself*): Blondie, she said! (*Looks around and moves so he can see himself in the mirror.*) Holy thunderbolt, I *am* a blond! It was so dark in there — I must have grabbed the wrong wig from the barber's table. What if Constantia sees me now?

Cypressa (*continuing her instructions to Emma*): And tell Constantia . . .

Titus: Oh-oh! She's already calling for her.

Cypressa: . . . to prepare my evening gown . . .

Titus (*to himself*): At least that will keep her busy for a while.

Emma: Yes, Mama. (*Mumbling while leaving*) That silly Constantia . . . trying to tease me . . . she knows my weakness for black hair!

Scene 17

Titus (*to himself*): She's an author — now, everyday words won't do . . . I'll have to dress up my speech in Sunday clothes . . .

CYPRESSA: And now for you, my good man . . .

TITUS (*bowing deeply*):   This is the moment I've anticipated and dreaded at the same time. I face it, if I may say so, with knee-shaking bravado and bold trembling.

CYPRESSA: You have little reason to be afraid. You seem to know how to behave, you have a passable appearance, and if you do your work . . . Tell me, where have you served before?

TITUS: My record is untarnished — I have served nowhere. This uniform contains an independent spirit ready to place itself in voluntary servitude for the first time.

CYPRESSA: And your father? Is he a gamekeeper, too?

TITUS: No, he has a quiet and peaceful occupation, the unbusiest of all business. His duties are heavenly, yet he is earthbound. He's held in bondage by the strictest master, yet he's free and independent, for he is the molder of his own existence — in short: he's dead.

CYPRESSA (*to herself*):   How lavishly he expresses in forty words what can be said in one — he's obviously gifted as an author. (*Aloud*) What is your education?

TITUS: I'm a product of the school of life. My education is tenuous but extremely widespread: a smattering of geography, a fraction of mathematics, a molecule of physics, just an idea of philosophy, a germ of medicine, and a pinch of the law.

CYPRESSA: How charming! You have learned much but not lost yourself in details. The mark of the true genius!

TITUS (*to himself*):   Ah, this explains why there are so many geniuses!

CYPRESSA: Your blond locks indicate a poetic soul. Did you get your hair from your mother's or your father's side?

TITUS: Neither. It's sheer coincidence.

CYPRESSA: The longer we talk the more I'm convinced that you're meant to wear a uniform. You're not cut out to be my servant.

TITUS: What? Dashed? Quashed? Smashed?

CYPRESSA: Not at all. I'm a writer and need someone to help me, not as a mere copyist but as a secretary, a consultant. That will be your job.

TITUS (*happily surprised*): Mine? Does Your Ladyship really think that I have it in me, this intellectual midwifery?

CYPRESSA: I have no doubts. The position happens to be open . . . I just had to let a young man go — a scholar, highly recommended, but unfortunately he had a touch of red in his hair. It gave me the shivers — I couldn't help it.

TITUS: I can't help it either . . . (*Quickly*) that I'm blond, I mean.

CYPRESSA: Well, a head of hair like yours certainly won't harm your career, young man. Now you take off that servant uniform. I expect company tonight and want to present you as my new secretary.

TITUS: If I take off this uniform I'll have to put on my old clothes which are a uniform, too — the uniform of poverty: a patched coat with worn cuffs.

CYPRESSA: That can easily be helped. Go in there . . . (*Pointing to the right*) you will find the wardrobe of my late husband. He had about your figure. Select what you need.

TITUS (*to himself*): Again the suit of a late lamented! (*Bowing*) Thank you, Your Ladyship! (*To himself, while leaving*) Today I'm dressing my way through an entire rummage sale.

(*Exits right.*)

Scene 18

CYPRESSA: The young man is dizzy from the heights to which I've lifted him. What will he say when I open for him the gates of heaven itself by reading him my poetry!

CONSTANTIA (*entering excitedly, through the center*): Shameful! That's what I call it: shameful!

CYPRESSA: What is it?

CONSTANTIA: I must complain about Mademoiselle Emma. It's shameful to carry a joke that far. She said I lied to her about the new gamekeeper's hair. First I thought she was having sport with me; but in the end she called me a dumbbell.

CYPRESSA: I'll reprimand her. By the way, the young man no longer is a gamekeeper. I made him my personal secretary, and expect everyone to show him the respect that goes with that position.

CONSTANTIA: Secretary! I'm delighted that he has pleased Your Ladyship. The black dress-coat of a secretary will beautifully match his hair.

CYPRESSA: What are you talking about?

CONSTANTIA: About his gorgeous black hair.

CYPRESSA: Don't be silly. I never saw a more beautiful blond.

CONSTANTIA: It pleases Your Ladyship to jest, too. I saw with my own eyes . . .

CYPRESSA: My eyes are just as own as yours.

CONSTANTIA: And Your Ladyship calls *that* blond?

CYPRESSA: What else?

CONSTANTIA: I beg your pardon, Your Ladyship, but I call it the pitchest pitch black I ever saw.

CYPRESSA: Don't be ridiculous. He's as blond as an angel.

CONSTANTIA: Heaven save us! Someone has bewitched us all!

CYPRESSA: Here he comes. See for yourself — is that dark or fair?

Scene 19

TITUS (*from right, in black dress-coat, breeches, silk stockings, and shoes*):   Here I am, Your Ladyship. (*Sees Constantia and shrinks back.*)

CONSTANTIA (*astonished*): How is that possible?

CYPRESSA (*to Constantia*): In the future I won't stand for such nonsense.

CONSTANTIA: But I only said what . . .

CYPRESSA: Enough. I want to hear no more.

TITUS (*to Cypressa*): Your Ladyship is upset? May I be of help?

CYPRESSA: Imagine — my maid here said your hair was black.

TITUS: Blackest slander and of the deepest dye!

CONSTANTIA: I'm losing my mind!

CYPRESSA: Never mind your mind. What counts is that I'm losing my patience. Go and lay out my clothes!

CONSTANTIA: I can only repeat . . .

CYPRESSA (*angrily*): And I repeat: go!

CONSTANTIA (*as if swallowing a big lump*): Mercy on us! Now the roosters will start laying eggs!

(*Exits center.*)

Scene 20

CYPRESSA: The person has gone mad!

TITUS (*to himself*): I feel like a shipwrecked sailor on a plank: to survive, I have to push off the others. (*Aloud*) Your Ladyship, I'm not surprised.

CYPRESSA: Why? Has she given you other indications?

TITUS: Well, indications is a weak word for what she's given me. I don't care to talk about it, but I dislike that sort of thing. She always looks at me as if . . . she talks to me as though . . . she behaves like . . . well, I just dislike that sort of thing.

CYPRESSA: She'll pack up, today!

TITUS: But what really shocks me is that all this time she

and this wigmaker . . . it reflects on the good reputation of the house.

CYPRESSA: Is he chasing her?

TITUS: Yes, and I'd have thought that at her age the only one who'd chase her was Father Time.

CYPRESSA (*amused*): Yes, she's rather in her declining years.

TITUS: I beg your pardon, Your Ladyship, but the only one in this house who is in her declining years is you.

CYPRESSA: What? How dare you — ?

TITUS: Oh, everybody knows that a woman is in her declining years only before she's thirty — after that she seldom declines.

CYPRESSA: How very clever. So, Constantia and that hairdresser . . .

TITUS: I don't want to talk about it.

CYPRESSA: I don't want to hear about it. What is it? It's my duty to know.

TITUS: It's my sad duty to tell. He . . . (*Looks around, then steps forward and whispers in her ear.*)

CYPRESSA (*thrilled*): No!

TITUS: Yes!

CYPRESSA: Anything else?

TITUS: Well, he also . . . (*Whispers again.*)

CYPRESSA (*gaping*): I'll never let this man touch my hair again!

TITUS: I'm sorry to see him go. But what I really didn't want to talk about is Flora, the gardener.

CYPRESSA: Is she immoral, too?

TITUS: Oh, no, on the contrary — she proposed marriage to me.

CYPRESSAS She'll leave today.

TITUS: I don't like to tattle like this, but . . .

CYPRESSA: I'm glad you told me. Write the three notes of dismissal right away.

TITUS: No, I can't do that. My first duty must not be so cruel.

CYPRESSA: Young man, your noble heart does you honor!

Scene 21

EMMA (*entering from the left*): Mama, I have to complain about Constantia. She forced me, by her stubborn behavior, to call her a dumbbell.

CYPRESSA: You will dismiss her today. Constantia in person, Flora and the wigmaker in writing.

EMMA: Yes, Mama.

TITUS (*pretending to be surprised*): Mama?

CYPRESSA: Yes, this is my daughter Emma.

TITUS: No — that's not possible!

CYPRESSA: Why not?

TITUS: It doesn't add up in years.

CYPRESSA (*very flattered*): Oh yes, it does.

TITUS: Such a young lady — and a grown-up daughter? No, I can't believe it — a distant sister, perhaps, a remote cousin twice removed. If Your Ladyship did have a daughter she could be only — at the very most — about that big. (*Indicates the size of a baby.*)

CYPRESSA: Yet, it's true. One conserves oneself.

TITUS: Oh, I know what conservation can do. But that would be ultra-conservatism!

CYPRESSA (*smiling benevolently*): Well, my droll young man, I now have to go and get ready for my guests. Come with me, Emma . . . (*To Titus*) See you soon.

TITUS (*as if overcome by emotion*): Oh yes, soon! (*Pretends to be upset by this outburst, bowing, in submissive tone*) Soon, I mean to say, to start out with my duties . . .

CYPRESSA (*smiling*): Adieu!

(*Exits left with Emma.*)

Scene 22

TITUS (*alone*): I'm in luck! All of a sudden I'm in luck.
I'm not used to people liking me. If all your life people slap
you down and suddenly you're able to charm them, that's
a new experience that changes not only you but the whole
world — human beings begin to look human and you can't
help suspect that some of them may have a heart, hidden
somewhere, and perhaps even a soul which is even harder
to find because it's behind the heart. Imagine — I'm now
one of them: I can talk to them, joke with them, work for
them, live in the same house with them — it's hard to
believe. I was used to hiding my feelings when my luck
was bad — but it's not so easy to hide good luck — every
breath becomes a trumpet, every motion a drumbeat:
"Look here, see this colossal bliss!" And all this change
took place since this morning — within the span of four or
five hours! Yes, time is a busy tailor who is doing all the
alterations in the shop of life. Sometimes the work goes
fast, sometimes slow, but it gets done, all the same — everything in the world gets altered.

SONG

A beauty turns down twelve proposals of marriage,
Including eight owners of horses with carriage.
Two string themselves up by their necks, for her sake,
Three blow out their brains, four jump in a lake,
And one Japanese commits harakiri.
But eighteen years later our dearie is weary:
Now *she* wants to marry, her boyfriends do not —
    Time changes a lot, yes, time changes a lot.

A rich man is fussy, has a cook and a valet,
And nothing is quite good enough for his palate.
He goes to the Alps for his milk and his trout,
Even Brussels will *not* do for *his* Brussels sprout.
He travels, in search of fried ants and frogs' legs,
And, in Africa, looking for crocodile eggs,
He ends up in the pot of the chief Hottentot —
  Yes, time changes a lot.

An opera singer — a smash hit was she,
Even hearing her hiccups they paid her a fee.
The envy left all of her colleagues depressed,
Even nightingales sometimes turned green in their nest.
Her C was so high it could shatter a glass
But seven years later it sounded like brass.
Her bust is still opera, but her voice is now shot —
  Yes, time changes a lot.

In the golden old days when a boyfriend felt brave,
He dragged his true love by her hair to his cave.
In the best of tradition of Adam's and Eve's
He gave her a wardrobe of newly-picked leaves.
"Mind the kids and the fire, and do all that I say,
While I go with the fellows a-hunting today."
"I'll obey you, my master," she said, "to the dot."
  Yes, times sure have changed — and a hell of a lot.

(*Exits.*)

Scene 23

SPONGE (*entering with several ladies and gentlemen*): Oh
yes, I'm looking forward to this evening. A literary tea is

my favorite beverage — it's the most nourishing brand of all teas.

GUEST: Every caramel comes with an ode, every fudge is wrapped in a sonnet . . .

Scene 24

CYPRESSA (*entering*): Welcome, ladies and gentlemen.

SPONGE (*bowing*): And the Muse herself is pouring . . .

GUEST: The air is fragrant — with poetry.

CYPRESSA: Please be seated.

(*All sit down at the table.*)

TITUS (*entering from the right*): Is it all right if I . . . ?

CYPRESSA: You're just in time. (*Presenting him*) My new secretary.

GUESTS: Delighted . . . enchanted . . .

CYPRESSA (*to Titus*): Please sit down. (*Titus sits down.*) This young man is going to read to you from my memoirs at our next soirée.

GUESTS: Ah . . . charming . . .

SPONGE: It's a pity Your Ladyship didn't write for the theater . . .

CYPRESSA: Who knows — I might try it sometime.

TITUS: I hear it's very simple — if you pick the right subject.

CYPRESSA: And what would that be?

TITUS: Love. It's the most original subject for a play, and I happen to know how it all got started. Creation, after creating man, which was a tragedy, tried its hand in a little comedy called "Love." It was an immediate smash hit, with many curtain calls and rave notices — so, the inevitable happened.

CYPRESSA: What was that?

TITUS: Creation got carried away and wrote a sequel called "Marriage." But as often happens with sequels, there just wasn't the interest.

SPONGE: How true!

TITUS: And consider the practical side: Love is cheap to produce — only two characters, no extras, any scenery will do, and the less lighting the better. But Marriage — just think of the cast of characters: a wife, a husband, a maid, a cook, servants, children, and a lot of extras, particularly if the wife is pretty. And the scenery: a salon, a ballroom, expensive restaurants . . . And the wardrobe — you know the bill a wife can run up! The language, too, is much coarser here — no, no, stay away from the sequel!

CYPRESSA (*to the lady next to her*): Well, what do you think of my new secretary?

Scene 25

FLORA (*enters from middle, crying*): Your Ladyship, please excuse me, but . . .

GUESTS: What happened? The gardener! She's crying!

TITUS (*alarmed*): How can I wiggle out of this?

FLORA (*to Cypressa*): I can't believe that I'm dismissed. I haven't done anything . . .

CYPRESSA: I don't have to account to you for my decisions.

FLORA (*seeing Titus*): What's this? He's blond?

CYPRESSA: The hair of my secretary is no concern of yours.

Scene 26

CONSTANTIA (*entering weeping with Emma, through the middle*): No, it can't be.

EMMA: I only carried out Mama's orders.

CONSTANTIA: Am I dismissed?

GUESTS: What? She, too?

CONSTANTIA: Your Ladyship, I'd never have expected that.
Without a reason . . .

SPONGE: What did she do?

CONSTANTIA: It's all because of the secretary's hair.

CYPRESSA: Nonsense. That has nothing to do with it. (*To
her guests*) By the way, what do you think of a person
who insists on calling this man's hair black? I ask you: is
it blond or isn't it?

CONSTANTIA: He is black.

FLORA: Yes, I know he's black.

Scene 27

MARQUIS (*entering through the center*): And I tell you he's
neither black nor blond. He's red!

GUESTS: Red?

TITUS (*desperate*): Well, hell! Now all is lost! (*Getting up
and tossing his wig into the middle of the stage*) Yes,
I'm red!

GUESTS (*in confusion*): What? Red? Oh, no!

CYPRESSA: Heaven forbid!

CONSTANTIA (*to Titus*): How disgusting you look!

FLORA (*to Titus*): And this beetroot wanted to marry me?

MARQUIS (*to Titus*): Wanted to get us all fired — eh?

CYPRESSA (*to Titus*): You are a fraud who spread false-
hoods about my most faithful servants! Out, go, or I'll call
the police!

TITUS (*to Cypressa*): Don't worry, I'm going . . .

GUESTS: Out!

TITUS (*resigned*): The rise and fall of the Roman Emperor

Titus! (*Exits slowly with lowered head. Guests in disarray;
Lady Cypressa affects a fainting spell; Mr. Sponge fans her.
Scene ends in general confusion.*)

CURTAIN

ACT THREE

(Lady Cypressa's garden. Same scene as at the beginning of Act Two.)

Scene 1

(Titus enters alone from behind the wing of the mansion.)

TITUS *(gloomily)*: The sweet home of my hopes has burned down, without insurance, my shares of good luck have dropped out of sight, and the figure of my cash is the fattest and roundest of all digits — zero. I'm back to my old belief that earth is a heavenly body on which most of us lead a hellish life. And why? Because people have no imagination — or they would realize how a man feels who is a man just like everybody else except that he has a different color of hair. They are not bad people — most of them are not, yet there is so much misery in the world because all of these millions of good people are nothing more than just good people. Well, I'm no worse off than when I started out — in fact, I profited by a good suit.

Scene 2

GEORGE *(coming quickly from behind the mansion)*: The Lady sent me after you. She wants you to leave all her things here — coat, breeches, shoes, everything.

TITUS: My dear man, you're on a most unpopular mission.

GEORGE: Never mind. Just leave the clothes here.

TITUS: Suppose I had skipped town?

GEORGE: We have laws. Our coppers catch all the tramps.

TITUS: Or suppose, my dear man, I forget about laws and lammed you one . . .

GEORGE: Help! Help!

TITUS: I said, "suppose." If you say suppose it's not against any laws.

GEORGE (*calling into the gardener's cottage*): Poponseed!

POPONSEED (*from inside*): What is it?

GEORGE (*opening the door and calling inside*): This tramp here . . . see that he puts on his old clothes.

POPONSEED (*as above*): Aye, aye.

TITUS (*to George*): You're a charming fellow.

GEORGE: Flattery won't get you anywhere. Off with you, and leave the good clothes in here. Understand?

(*Exits.*)

Scene 3

TITUS (*alone*): Oh yes, I understand it all. I had a little success, and it not only turned my head, it wrung my neck, and now bad luck is coming for a visit. I meant to receive it in a black coat and silken stockings but bad luck says: "I've known you all your life, don't bother dressing up, your old clothes will do."

POPONSEED (*from inside*): What's keeping you?

TITUS: I'm coming.

(*Exits into the cottage.*)

Scene 4

SALOME (*entering from left with Bung*): You promise you won't do him any harm?

BUNG: I told you a thousand times, I'm only doing what the master brewer told me. He speaks for the entire guild and he's the only man I listen to.

SALOME: And what did he tell you?

BUNG: He told me, "That's what you get for not paying any attention to the boy. Now he's taken off and will disgrace your family." That's why I'm looking for him.

SALOME: You don't want to get him arrested?

BUNG: I'd love to, but the master brewer told me, "That would disgrace your family."

SALOME: Oh, come now, your own flesh and blood —

BUNG: Your flesh and blood can be a pain in the neck if it sprouts red hair.

SALOME: Is that a crime?

BUNG: Red hair is the sign of a sly temperament, a slippery character — and it spoils the image of the family. Of course, everybody in the family is dead except me and him, but they all had brown hair, there wasn't a spark of fire in them — and then this boy had the nerve to be born a redhead.

SALOME: That's no reason to let your own nephew starve. If you have something yourself, that is.

BUNG: What I have, I owe to my brains. My parents didn't leave me a penny. But I figured things out.

SALOME: How's that?

BUNG: It wasn't simple. First, Cousin Alois died and left me ten thousand thalers. That set me thinking. I figured, if more of my family would pay their last debt, I'd be sitting pretty. And what do you know? Four weeks later, Aunt Mitzi cashes in her chips and comes across with thirty thousand. The next summer Uncle Fritz calls it quits to the tune of twenty thousand, and the winter after that, Cousin August gets his everlasting and treats me to forty thousand more — just as I figured it. And then I won eighteen thousand in the lottery.

SALOME: What? That, too?

BUNG: Yes, you mustn't get the idea that inheriting money is all there is to it. You must try other ways, too. That's using the old noddle.

SALOME: If you're so good at figuring, don't you figure that your day will come, too, and that Titus will inherit everything?

BUNG: Oh no, he won't. I can always find people more to my taste, so the redhead doesn't have to disgrace me by doing *me* the last honor.

SALOME: Then you'll do nothing for Titus?

BUNG: I'll do what the master brewer told me. I'm going to buy him a barber shop in Vienna, that will keep him out of mischief, give him a few thousand thalers so he'll not disgrace the family, then I'll call him a few names for being a redtop, and tell him to keep out of my hair.

SALOME: Then you *will* do something for him?

BUNG: I'll do what the master brewer told me.

SALOME (*sadly*): I'm happy for him but when he's no longer poor he'll really be lost to me. (*Sighing*) He is, anyway.

BUNG: What does he do up there in the mansion?

SALOME: I don't know for certain but he's wearing a pretty uniform all covered with gold braid.

BUNG: A servant's uniform! It's a disgrace for the family — a nephew of a beer salesman wearing a servant's uniform! Show me the way to him and I'll shake him out of it — quickly!

SALOME: But I'm telling you . . .

BUNG (*agitated*): Quick, I said. I owe a lot to my family!

(*Exits, driving Salome ahead of him across the stage.*)

Scene 5

FLORA (*entering, left*):   Holla, Poponseed! Poponseed!
POPONSEED (*entering, from cottage*):   What is it?
FLORA: The tramp is gone, I hope?
POPONSEED: No, he's putting on his old clothes.
FLORA: Tell him to hurry.
POPONSEED (*maliciously*):   Do you want to invite him to one
of those cozy dinners for two where I'm not wanted?
FLORA: Go get lost!
POPONSEED: Now you can have him all to yourself. The
Lady's maid will let you have him.
FLORA: Shut up and send him on his way.
POPONSEED (*calling into the cottage*):   You there, hurry up
and get on your way.
TITUS (*from inside*):   I'm done.

Scene 6

TITUS (*enters in old clothes from cottage*):   Here I am.
FLORA: That's the wrong place for you to be.
TITUS: The gardener lady who gave me the brush! How
would you like to give me a little something else on my
way?
FLORA: What? For the dirty trick you played on me you
want me to *give* you something? I'd rather check to see
you haven't *taken* anything! (*Looks at him with contempt
and exits into the cottage.*)
POPONSEED: Yes, one never knows! (*Also looks at Titus contemptuously.*) You red blockhead!

(*Exits to the cottage.*)

Scene 7

Titus (*alone*): Impertinent folk! I shouldn't be surprised if illusions leave the heart only slowly, in single droplets. I deserve to be trampled on — I did the same thing to others when I was on top. I stabbed Flora in the back, that wig-maker who tried to help me, and even Constantia. I never did more than talk about them — but I should have known from my own experience that the tongue is the deadliest of all blunt instruments. A few hours ago I had a whole mansion at my disposal, and for tonight I don't even have a bundle of hay to sleep on.

George (*from behind the mansion, politely*): Mr. Titus! Mr. Titus!

Titus: I'm going.

George: I'm glad I still caught you. You're wanted at the mansion.

Titus: I — wanted? For what?

George: I don't know but the Lady's maid wishes to talk to you.

Titus: What? Constantia?

George: The Lady, too, wants to see you once more. Be up there in half an hour.

Titus: I'll be there. What do I have to lose?

George: Very well, Mr. Titus, the Lady will be expecting you.

(*Bows and leaves.*)

Scene 8

Titus (*alone*): Is he pulling my leg? Or did Lady Cypressa get a conscience indigestion after she chewed me to

pieces? Conscience is a funny material . . . very elastic —
today it's hardly big enough to cover a molehill, and tomorrow it will spread over a whole mountain. Has the
Lady's conscience forced her to tolerate my red-headed
presence? Wait . . . ! I'll make it easier on her eyes . . .
(*Reaching into his pocket*) I still have the gray wig of the
departed gardener . . . (*Pulls it out.*) I'll put it on for my
last visit. Black and blond and red people have at least
that much in common that they all turn gray in the end.
I'm not cheating, just giving them a glimpse of things to
come. Maybe the gray wig will bring more lasting luck.

(*Exits left.*)

Scene 9

FLORA (*running from the cottage, to Poponseed*): I saw it,
he took it. Stop, thief! Come, Poponseed, run after him!
POPONSEED: It's not worth the bother.
FLORA: He stole the wig of my beloved husband — to me
it's full of memories!
POPONSEED: Oh, come on, it's full of moths!
FLORA: Don't argue — what's the idea?
POPONSEED: I haven't had an idea in years.
FLORA: Run, I tell you! Quick!
POPONSEED (*walking off slowly*): I'll do my best but I doubt
if I can catch him.

Scene 10

FLORA (*alone, angrily*): I have a good mind to have him
arrested, that bummel!
GEORGE (*entering from the left*): What's bothering you?

FLORA: Oh, that good-for-nothing, Titus.

GEORGE: Well — wait a minute. Respect where respect is due. I called him names too, but now it turns out that he has a filthy rich uncle who'll buy him a barber shop in the city and give him a heap of money.

FLORA: You don't say!

GEORGE: The Lady sent me after him, to ask him back to the mansion — and I had to say "Mister" to him. Respect where respect is due.

(*Exits.*)

Scene 11

FLORA (*alone*): Well, well — that throws a different light on everything. I bet Constantia is reconsidering and has asked Lady Cypressa to help her land him. I know Constantia — she'll take a second look at that redtop now that he has a rich uncle. I may have been a little rough on Titus myself for something over which, after all, he has no control. (*Looking to the left*) There he is still! Hey, Titus, Titus!

TITUS (*from the left, the gray wig in his hand*): Yes, I know, it has sentimental value for you. There, you can have it back, your gray wig.

FLORA: Oh, not at all, keep it. Although I don't know why you want to be gray at your age.

TITUS: Woman, if you'd been a redtop all your life, you'd consider any color an improvement.

FLORA: I'm afraid I was a bit rude before.

TITUS: It wasn't so bad, you only called me a tramp and a thief.

FLORA: I could kick myself.

TITUS: Say, how about this sudden rash of sisterly love?

FLORA: Well, the way I see it, it's the duty of a Christian to do good deeds, even to his enemies. But that doesn't mean you can't call people names and wish them a little bad luck — it doesn't follow that it'll turn out that way. No one is without faults, you know. You have to take the good with the bad.

TITUS: That's true. Even a person who has one leg too short, also has a longer leg — and, I guess, everyone who has a shortage in his character must also have some bigness in him, somewhere.

FLORA: I was just thinking the same thing about your hair, too. After all, no men are without faults, so the choice is between having no man or taking one with faults.

TITUS: Flora, gardener, you're giving me back my faith in mankind! I've got to pinch myself: I'm Titus, the beetroot, with no talisman to cover up my head — and yet I'm being treated like a human being!

DUET

TITUS: Madame Flora!

FLORA: Mister Titus!

TITUS: What's the bond that may unite us?

FLORA: Never underestimate
Any woman, keep this straight.

TITUS   (*bowing to her*): If I underestimate
It's her age, perhaps her weight.

FLORA: A girl who is clever looks over the field.

TITUS: A man with red hair — may he hope he appealed?

FLORA: The chances are slim that they'll get intertwined.

TITUS: I already had lost all my faith in mankind.

FLORA: A girl has to pick the best deal she can find.

TITUS: I already had lost all my faith in mankind.

FLORA: But there are exceptions to every rule.

TITUS: I've heard this before, I learned it in school.
FLORA: A girl is entitled to changing her mind.
TITUS: Are you giving me back now my faith in mankind?
FLORA: Our love, on occasion, can be colorblind.
TITUS: You're giving me back all my faith in mankind!

FLORA: Mister Titus!
TITUS: Madame Flora!
         Come and be my faith restorer.
FLORA: Conscience has turned on the heat,
         Tells me that I mustn't cheat.
TITUS: Is it conscience and the heat?
         Or did Flora get cold feet?
FLORA: Your mind is like lightning — it's quick but it's crooked.
TITUS   (*clawing the air to scare her*):
         I'm a blackheaded monster — although I don't look it.
         I'm a redheaded devil with a vampire mind.
FLORA: O horror, I'm losing my faith in mankind.
TITUS: I am growing a tail sprouting out from behind —
FLORA: I'm done for — I've lost all my faith in mankind.
TITUS: It may not be true — was perhaps I maligned?
FLORA: That indeed would restore all my faith in mankind.
TITUS: On beer, not on blood, I have wined and have dined.
FLORA: You're giving me back all my faith in mankind.

TITUS: Madame Flora!
FLORA: Mister Titus!
         Singing gives me tonsillitis.
TITUS: But in our day and age
         Opera is the greatest rage.
FLORA: Everybody sings like birdies
         Wagner's arias or Verdi's.
TITUS   (*parodying opera style*):
         O villainous woman, accursèd and wretchèd!

FLORA: I'm a victim of lechery, I swear, I was lechèd.
         The King himself was it who after me pined.
TITUS: The King made me lose all my faith in mankind.
         If His Majesty ordered, obedience is blind.
FLORA: My hero has lost all his faith in mankind.
         But hark, my beloved, and please stop your barking.
TITUS: Speak up, cursèd woman, speak up — I am harking.
FLORA: A purse full of ducats the King left behind.
TITUS: Such a gift gives me back all my faith in mankind.
         The ducats are gold and you haven't declined?
FLORA: Thank heavens, he's recaptured his faith in mankind!

FLORA: Mister Titus!
TITUS: Madame Flora!
         Times have changed, my dear signora.
FLORA: Modern music blasts and blares.
TITUS: Opera is reserved for squares.
FLORA: Radio, hi-fi, and TV
         Bring us cacosymphony.
TITUS: The boys bang the drum and they strum the guitar.
FLORA: The audience — it screams and it faints — it's bizarre.
TITUS: They sing "yeah, yeah, yeah," all go out of their mind.
FLORA: It's enough to lose faith in the whole of mankind.
TITUS: The musicians' long hair makes them practically blind.
FLORA: I already have lost all my faith in mankind.
TITUS: But the Viennese waltz is still king of the ball.
FLORA: My faith in mankind is restored after all.
TITUS: Surviving the twist are wine, women, and song.
FLORA: My faith in mankind is again very strong.

ENCORE

FLORA: Mister Titus!
TITUS: Madame Flora!

Come, and let's sing an encora.
FLORA (*to the audience*):
Your applause, this must delight us,
Even goes to redhead Titus.
TITUS: Yes, this makes a man feel good:
Superstition's dead, touch wood.
FLORA: No longer will prejudice hang on a hair.
TITUS: It has become skin-deep, that's progress, I swear.
FLORA: A prejudiced man finds it hard to unwind.
TITUS: I'd already lost all my faith in mankind.
FLORA: A man who looks different is still left behind.
TITUS: It sure makes me lose all my faith in mankind.
FLORA: Today all the redheads can work where they wish.
TITUS: A redheaded girl is considered a *dish*.
FLORA: That's progress since Nestroy's time, keep that in mind.
TITUS: You've given me back all my faith in mankind.
FLORA: We've made a good start, let's not keep it confined:
TITUS: You've given me back all my faith in mankind.

Scene 12

(*Room in the mansion with arches and glass doors
in the center leading to a terrace and moonlit garden. Doors left and right. Lights on tables on both
sides.*)

CONSTANTIA (*alone*): I didn't think that wigmaker had it in
him. All of a sudden he turns up his nose at me and says
goodbye forever. This could crush an ordinary widow but I,
thank heavens, only need to cast a glance, and another man,
Mr. Titus, is at my feet. I only hope the Lady can get that
old beerocrat of an uncle to make Titus his heir.

Scene 13

CYPRESSA (*entering from left*):   Constantia!

CONSTANTIA: Your Ladyship?

CYPRESSA: It won't work.

CONSTANTIA: He won't do it?

CYPRESSA: I spent half an hour with the man but his water-tight soul is impenetrable. He'll buy Titus a shop but he won't make him his heir.

CONSTANTIA: What a miserable miser!

CYPRESSA: Don't look down on a miser — misers make wonderful persons to inherit from.

CONSTANTIA: I didn't think he would give Your Ladyship any trouble. I even called in the notary, to draft the papers. Let's try again, together.

CYPRESSA: If you want to . . . I've done you an injustice this morning and would like to make it up to you by an act of motherly guidance.

CONSTANTIA (*kissing her hand*):   Your Ladyship is extremely good to me.

CYPRESSA (*leaving with Constantia at left*):   I have little hope, though. Unless a meeting with his nephew will make a dent . . .

CONSTANTIA: Titus ought to be here at any moment.

(*Both leave left.*)

Scene 14

(*Titus enters through the glass door with George. He wears the gray wig with an old-fashioned queue.*)

TITUS: Can't you tell me . . . ?

GEORGE:⌐ Strict orders. (*Staring at him*) Why are you wearing a gray wig?

TITUS: If you don't tell me anything, I won't tell you anything. I was asked to come here, so I'm here. Go and announce me to Her Ladyship.

GEORGE: All right, all right. I will.

(*Exits left.*)

Scene 15

TITUS (*alone*): It'll sting a little here . . . (*Pointing at his heart*) to see Constantia again. But I only need to recall when she said "How disgusting you look!" Such a recollection is the best medicine for a soft spot in your head. The Lady's maid can remain an old maid, for all I care — I'm through with women! (*Enter George.*) Have you announced me?

GEORGE: No, Her Ladyship is in conference and must not be disturbed.

TITUS (*mimics him*): Her Ladyship is in conference . . .

GEORGE: You'll just have to wait. After a while I'll go and see if it's time to announce you.

(*Exits right.*)

Scene 16

TITUS: Oh, fiddledeedee, you uniformed serving machine! The Lady in conference? I should live so long! People all over the place get the silliest excuses thrown into their faces, and they're expected to swallow them politely.

Song

A man comes to see me, makes a touch for a buck.
He says: "I am starving, I've had such bad luck.
I'm looking for work but there's *no* vacancy.
My mother needs care and my wife has TB."
His breath smells of wine, and my feeling is strong:
   I should live so long!

"This thing has to stop," shouts the husband in rage.
Her eyelashes flutter like birds in a cage.
"You're jealous," she stammers, "and this makes you blind.
The man is in love with my soul and my mind.
We only read Shakespeare, we just play mah-jong."
   I should live so long!

A cigarette firm has found out by research
That to smoke is as safe as to sit in a church.
It is true, they acknowledge: some doctors believe
That smoking is harmful — but this is naïve:
For ten million customers cannot be wrong!
   They should live so long!

Encore

Three generals I see in my bright crystal ball
Who have moved from the front to the conference hall.
They've sent home the soldiers of their last platoon
And are taking together a trip to the moon.
Their names are Kotchenko, Jim Smith, and Li Wong —
   . . . so long!

                                            (*Exits.*)

Scene 17

CYPRESSA (*entering from left with Constantia*): I wonder what's keeping him . . .

CONSTANTIA: George said he'd be here . . .

TITUS (*entering right*): Your Ladyship is referring to me?

CYPRESSA: Ah, there you are. You'll be surprised to hear the news . . .

CONSTANTIA (*to Cypressa*): Your Ladyship . . . look — his hair!

CYPRESSA: What kind of masquerade is this?

TITUS (*pointing to his wig*): That's the only wig I could get my hands on. I'm wearing it to save Your Ladyship the upsetting experience of having to talk to a redhead.

CYPRESSA: Oh well, your shade of red is not too offensive . . .

TITUS: But the way you carried on . . .

CYPRESSA: Take that wig off. You have a visitor . . .

CONSTANTIA (*noticing Bung entering from the left*): Too late. He's here.

CYPRESSA (*to Bung*): Here's your nephew, Mr. Bung.

CONSTANTIA (*to Cypressa*): I don't have much hope for this cement-head — he's all mixed up and hardened to a rock!

(*Both leave.*)

Scene 18

TITUS (*surprised*): Uncle Bung! How did you get here?

BUNG: In a more honest way than you. Vanishing into thin air is not my way of traveling.

TITUS: Would be hard to do, anyway, for a man of your tonnage.

BUNG: You disgrace of the family! You black sheep! (*Peers at Titus' hair*) What's that? Gray hair?

TITUS (*embarrassed*): Well . . . you see . . .

BUNG: But you are a paprikahead!

TITUS: I was.

BUNG: And now?

TITUS: I'm gray.

BUNG: But that's impossible . . .

TITUS: Reality is the best proof of the possible.

BUNG: You're only twenty-six!

TITUS: I was, yesterday. But being abandoned by my only kinsman, and having to wander alone through the world, has aged me a thousand years. I've become gray overnight.

BUNG: Overnight?

TITUS: At seven sharp I leave home, an hour later I look into the mirror of the desperate, the river, and my hair is like a radish sprinkled with salt. I think it's the twilight, select my night's quarters — a ditch, with the fog for a blanket — and fall asleep again. In the morning, I look in the river again handful of my hair — it's gray. I blame the silvery moon and fall asleep again. In the morning, I look in the river again and the bright flame of yesterday has burned to ashes — I recognize the hair as mine only by the face that's hanging from it.

BUNG: That's unbelievable!

TITUS: Oh no, it's happened before. For instance, to a certain Belisarius — have you heard of him?

BUNG: Was he a beer salesman?

TITUS: No, he was a Roman general. His wife had the Senate scratch out his eyes.

BUNG: Women usually do that themselves.

TITUS: Well, this one used the legislative branch for it. Belisarius took it hard, and in three times twenty-four hours he was gray. Just think of it, Uncle, a Roman general needed three days for what I accomplished overnight — and you, Uncle, are the cause of this historical event!

BUNG (*very moved*): Titus, lad, flesh-and-blood . . . I don't know what's coming over me — I am the uncle of an historical event! (*Sobbing*) Nineteen years I haven't shed a tear, and now they come by the bucket. (*Dries his eyes.*)

TITUS: It's good for the old beer to come out!

BUNG (*spreading his arms*): Come here, ash-colored boy! (*Embraces Titus.*)

TITUS (*embracing Bung*): Uncle Bung! (*Suddenly draws back.*)

BUNG: Why are you bouncing off like a barrel on a staircase?

TITUS (*embarrassed, trying to keep the wig's tail out of Bung's reach*): You . . . eh . . . hurt me . . . with your ring.

BUNG: Don't be a sissy, lad! Back to your uncle's heart! (*Titus lifts the tail of the wig during the embrace with his right hand, to prevent it from being pulled by Bung.*) That's better. (*Letting Titus go*) I'll tell you what: so this ring won't hurt you any more . . . (*Pulls off a heavy signet ring from his finger and hands it to Titus.*) There you are. Now I want you to know that I'm going to take you back to Vienna, buy you a fine barber shop, and . . .

TITUS (*happily*): Uncle Bung!

BUNG: Look at your clothes . . . this coat . . . it's a disgrace. And I'll have to present you as my nephew to the Lady . . . and this other person . . .

TITUS (*scared*): What other person? A hairdresser?

BUNG: Hairdresser? (*Laughs with heavy-handed waggishness.*) No, lad, don't play tricks with me! My eyes are poor but I could see that she wasn't after your *hair*, that person. (*Takes a brush from the table.*) Let me clean you up a bit . . .

TITUS: What are you doing?

BUNG: I'm tidying up a natural phenomenon that slept in a ditch. I'm dusting a historical event — that's no disgrace, not even for a beer salesman. Turn around!

TITUS: No, no! Start in front!

BUNG (*brushing in front*):   Just imagine! Getting all gray worrying about the family. (*Moved*) I'm getting all flabby-hearted. It was I who left you in the ditch . . . Now turn.

TITUS (*in desperation*):   Uncle, would you believe that my worries about the family not only made my hair gray but also made me grow a queue?

> (*Bung has stopped brushing and taken out a hand-kerchief to blow his nose. He hasn't heard Titus' last remark.*)

BUNG: Look, Titus, lad. I've never had a boy to take care of . . . you are a good lad . . . you've taken it to heart because I was such a cold-hearted uncle. And why was I cold-hearted? Because you had red hair. But now you don't have red hair no more, so there's no reason to be cold-hearted. Even the master brewer would agree to that. You are my only kinsman, you are my nephew — you are as much as my son . . . I'll make you my sole heir!

TITUS: What?!

Scene 19

CYPRESSA (*entering with Constantia and notary*):   "Sole heir" . . . these are the words we've been waiting for.

CONSTANTIA: We knew your heart would tell you what to do. That's why we brought the notary along.

CYPRESSA: And he has brought the necessary papers.

BUNG: Good. Where are they?

> (*Notary pulls out papers and discusses them with Bung in the background.*)

TITUS (*to Cypressa, referring to Constantia*):   She's pushing my inheritance faster than I.

CYPRESSA (*to Titus*): You see how much this unselfish woman (*Pointing at Constantia*) acts in your best interest? She has confided in me and I'm ready to bless the bond which love has tied and gratitude will strengthen.

TITUS (*bows before her*): Women's styles may change but their designs remain the same.

BUNG: Everything's fine. Roll out the barrel!

(*Constantia and the notary lead him to the table with inkstand and quills. He sits down to sign.*)

TITUS (*to Constantia*): That he buys me a barber shop I can accept — he's my uncle. But to become his heir on a fraud — no! (*To Bung*) One moment, Uncle, let me . . .

BUNG: What? Are you still not satisfied?

Scene 20

FLORA (*entering through the center*): Your Ladyship, I've come . . .

CYPRESSA: At the wrong time.

FLORA: . . . to settle my account.

CYPRESSA: Didn't I tell you that you may stay?

FLORA: Yes but . . . I'm not sure now . . . I may marry and move to the city.

CYPRESSA: Marry? Whom?

FLORA: It's too early to say, but Mr. Titus . . .

CYPRESSA: What?

CONSTANTIA (*at the same time*): What impertinence!

BUNG (*to Titus*): To how many womenfolk have you promised marriage, in your desperation?

TITUS: Promised? None.

BUNG: Oh, I don't care. Marry who you want. You're my sole heir, you can support them all!

Scene 21

SALOME (*rushing in through the center*): Mr. Titus! Mr. Titus! (*She sees the crowd of people and freezes at the doorway, without noticing Flora.*)

CYPRESSA: What do *you* want?

SALOME (*shyly*): I beg your pardon . . .

CYPRESSA: How dare you break in here?

SALOME: I have a message from Madame gardener for Mr. Titus . . .

CYPRESSA: Flora needs no messenger. She's here.

SALOME (*noticing Flora*): Oh, yes, then she can tell him herself.

CYPRESSA: Tell what?

SALOME: Nothing. She's signaling me not to tell.

CYPRESSA: Come out with it. Speak up!

SALOME: Not as long as Madame gardener is signaling me . . .

CYPRESSA (*to Flora*): You stop that. (*To Salome*) Well . . . ?

SALOME (*embarrassed*): Madame gardener told Poponseed, and Poponseed told me to tell Mr. Titus . . .

CYPRESSA (*impatiently*): What?

SALOME: To give back her wi . . . (*Cypressa and Constantia try to restrain her.*) . . . her wig.

BUNG: What wig?

TITUS (*taking off the gray wig*): This one.

BUNG (*angrily*): What? You've had the nerve . . .

CONSTANTIA (*to Cypressa*): Now all is lost!

CYPRESSA (*to Constantia*): Quiet! (*To Titus*) That was a childish prank you tried to play on your distinguished uncle. But you didn't really think that a man of his brains would fall for it? He would have to be a real nitwit not to have seen through it right away. But as a man of wit . . .

TITUS: He played along and played a prank on *me*!

CYPRESSA (*to Bung*): Isn't that so?

BUNG (*perplexed*): Huh? Oh yes, yes, of course. I fooled him good, didn't I?

CYPRESSA (*to Titus*): And now it's up to you to ask his forgiveness.

CONSTANTIA (*to Titus*): A smart man like your uncle certainly won't deny you the inheritance just because the color of your hair happens to be red. (*To Bung*) Am I right?

BUNG (*as above*): Of course, oh yes.

TITUS (*to Constantia and Flora*): Now, wait a minute . . . there are a few things I have to say about this, too. One is, that I will not accept Uncle Bung's money. If he will buy me a barber shop — fine, that's all I need. I'll be very grateful for it. I need no inheritance, and I wish him a long and happy life of about three hundred years!

BUNG (*moved*): A person can sell a lot of beer in that time! You're a good lad, in spite of your red hair!

TITUS (*referring to Constantia and Flora*): Secondly, I will not marry anyone who will pardon red hair only when it's growing on the head of a sole heir. Neither will I marry anyone who looks at my fiery hair and sees it grow paler with every thousand thalers I inherit. I'll stick with the girl who cared for Titus before he had a talisman either on his head or in his pocketbook — and that, I believe, was the case with this one. (*Embraces the surprised Salome.*)

SALOME: What? Mr. Titus?

TITUS: Is yours, if you want him.

CYPRESSA (*icily cold*): Adieu! (*Exits indignantly at the left, followed by the notary.*)

CONSTANTIA: Her Ladyship wishes not to be disturbed any further! (*Exits.*)

FLORA (*to Titus, maliciously*): Congratulations! Birds of a feather flock together! (*Exits.*)

BUNG (*to Titus*): What about me? Don't I have any say about whom you marry?

TITUS (*with reference to Salome*): I know, Uncle, you don't like redheads. Almost no one likes them. And why? Because there are so few of them, because they're in the minority, because they're different. If there were lots of redheads, people wouldn't even notice them, they'd be acceptable. But we shall overcome: The solution to the problem is for redheads to multiply like rabbits, and you can be sure, Uncle, that Salome and I will do our share.

CURTAIN

Love Affairs
and Wedding Bells

(LIEBESGESCHICHTEN UND

HEIRATSSACHEN)

A Farce with Songs, in Three Acts

Playbill of the first performance of *Love Affairs and Wedding Bells*
(*Liebesgeschichten und Heiratssachen*) at the Theater an der Wien,
March 23, 1843, presented as a benefit for the playwright. Nestroy
did his utmost to build up his part in order to accomplish a virtuoso
performance. In spite of this, the play was only a mild success and
Nestroy registered no more than forty-two performances in twelve
years. It was not printed during his lifetime, and no picture of the
early productions exists. (The illustration is the left half of a double-
spread. The right half, containing the date, announces a Hungarian
dancing group in the Theater in der Leopoldstadt, under the same
management.)

Only in recent years was *Love Affairs and Wedding Bells* rediscovered as a classical comedy of errors that contains some of Nestroy's most biting witticisms. The photograph, from a performance at the Volkstheater in Vienna shows the two main characters, the Nestroy part (Moon) and the Scholz part (Lard), hatching one of the many plots in the play.

CHARACTERS

Herr von Lard,
  former sausage maker, a *nouveau riche*
Fritzi, his daughter
Ulrike, his distant relative
Lucia Thistle, his sister-in-law
Ferdinand Buchner
Marquis François de Vincelli
Alfred, his son
Moon, an unemployed adventurer
Innkeeper
Innkeeper's wife
Philippina, maidservant of Lard
Kling, manservant of the Marquis
Snail, a coachman
First Servant of Lard
Second Servant of Lard
Policeman
Policemen, and servants at the inn

Time and place: Mid-nineteenth-century Austria

ACT ONE

(Dining room in the Silver Stallion Inn)

Scene 1

ALFRED (*sitting at a table*): Now the address ...

INNKEEPER: I know it's none of my business to ask ...

ALFRED: An indication that you shouldn't.

INNKEEPER: But I can't help wondering why you always come here to write your letters.

ALFRED: An indication that I have no time to do it on my job.

INNKEEPER: And why don't you post your letters yourself instead of giving them to the coachman?

ALFRED: An indication that I'm in no hurry.

INNKEEPER: You come here twice a week, order wine, never drink it, toss half a thaler on the table ... such doings make a man like me curious.

ALFRED: An indication that you see your weakness — the surest indication that you'll overcome it. (*The rattling of a coach is heard from outside.*) Here's the coach now. Get hold of the coachman and send him in.

INNKEEPER: All right, Sir. (*Muttering as he walks out*) Strange fellow. Can't figure him out — him and his letter-writing.

(*Exits.*)

Scene 2

ALFRED (*alone, addressing the letter*): "To His Excellency, the Marquis François de Vincelli." Oh Father, I hate to cheat like this — but I can't let you meet Ulrike here — it's not her fault that fate has tossed her into this family of disgusting plebeians!

SNAIL (*entering through the center*): Your Excellency! Does Your Excellency have the letter ready?

ALFRED: Here it is. You know what to do.

SNAIL: As always. Post it when I get to Milan.

ALFRED: But not before Saturday — I predated it by six days.

SNAIL: That's the ticket! The old man gets it in Vienna, sees the Milan postmark . . .

ALFRED: All right, all right. I just hope you're as discreet as you are smart.

SNAIL: Discretion runs in the family. Next week my brother will come through here, same time, same station . . .

ALFRED: I'll have another letter ready. (*Gives him money.*)

SNAIL: At your service. Well, I'm off. I have brought my passenger, picked up my letter . . .

Scene 3

FERDINAND BUCHNER (*entering with Innkeeper*): I need a room for one week.

INNKEEPER (*to a servant, very obsequiously*): Jepp, get the room next to the baron's ready for the gentleman this instant.

SERVANT: I'll bring in the rest of the luggage.

FERDINAND: This suitcase is all I have.

INNKEEPER (*sobering up; sizing up the situation; off-hand to servant*): Show the fellow the attic room.

(*Exits.*)

Scene 4

ALFRED: Well, what do I see? Ferdinand Buchner!

FERDINAND: Oh, Chevalier . . . or Marquis . . . Oh, what's the difference for old schoolmates! Only you're a Highness now, and I'm a penniless Lowness, that's the difference.

ALFRED: What do you mean? How can the son of the most prosperous merchant in Vienna be penniless? Have you been cut off?

FERDINAND: No, Father was. His creditors took all his money, and the most insistent one took him.

ALFRED: The most insistent?

FERDINAND: Death. With his money gone, my father could not keep up his interest. When the fellow with the hour-glass showed up, Father was glad to go with him. The news reached me in London. I was seeing the world but what was there to see? The world turned out to be just what I'd imagined.

ALFRED: Then you didn't see it. No one imagines the world as it really is. How much do you have left?

FERDINAND: The trip from London took it all.

ALFRED: What are you going to do?

FERDINAND: Get married.

ALFRED: And live on what?

FERDINAND: My wife's money.

ALFRED: You don't mean that!

FERDINAND: No, it isn't the way it sounds. When we met she had nothing and I was rich. In the meantime, her father has inherited a fortune, and I've lost mine. But when you're in love, the question who has the money makes about as much difference as whether a mosquito is lighting on your right or your left ear. We settled everything before I started traveling. She said yes, and her father agreed. So now all we need to do is to live happily ever after.

ALFRED: And *you* traveled to get to know the world?

FERDINAND: For almost a year.

ALFRED (*whistles in astonishment*): You really *did* waste your money! Where is your fiancée now?

FERDINAND: Right in this village. She's the daughter of Florian Lard, the sausage maker. They used to live in a room behind the butcher shop but now, I understand, he's bought himself a title and a mansion.

ALFRED: What? Fritzi Lard?

FERDINAND: You know her?

ALFRED: I've been secretary to Lard for a couple of months.

FERDINAND: I smell romance. You aren't in love with Fritzi, are you?

ALFRED: No, my heart belongs to Ulrike, Fritzi's cousin, who is living with the Lards now.

FERDINAND: And your father?

ALFRED: Will explode when he hears about it.

FERDINAND: What will you do?

ALFRED: All I can to get his permission.

FERDINAND: What if he refuses?

ALFRED: Then I'm ready to sacrifice everything — my inheritance, my future, even my father's love.

FERDINAND: A romantic, like myself. I like that. Let's go to the mansion together.

ALFRED: It's better if we pretend not to know each other. Lard is stupid but suspicious. I'll go first, you follow later.

FERDINAND: You're right, that's smarter. But I'll go with you part of the way. You must tell me all about my Fritzi.

(*Both leave.*)

Scene 5

MOON (*entering from the left*):

SONG

They tell me, a man must not live just on bread,
But I do it on crust, and I'm always ahead.
I am quick as a dart, when I run into debt,
But for paying them back, I slow down and forget.
I am what they call a professional moocher,
I've plenty of past, but not much of a future,
Yet I eat and I drink, with no sweat on my brow —
   And no one knows how.

The optimist often proclaims with a cheer:
"The best of all possible worlds is right here!"
The pessimist looks at the hullabaloo
And admits he's afraid this might really be true.
Some people are sure that the best man will win,
While others just know you must bear it and grin.
Some believe in a doomsday, some in pie in the sky —
   And no one knows why.

A millionaire banker of three score and ten
Takes a girl in her teens when he marries again.
She adores the old man, entertains all his friends.
The husband gets tired but her fun never ends.
After one year of marriage, O blessing and joy!
She gives birth to a baby, a fine little boy.
His friends say that Dad must be proud of the two —
   But no one knows who.

ENCORE

In Metternich's era, to say what you think
Meant playing with fire and courting the clink.
The censor, of course, is abolished today,
You say what you want now in any which way —
Unless you insist upon keeping your job,
Being friends with your neighbors, and pleasing the mob.
True freedom of speech? It will come to all men —
　　But no one knows when.

If you're a man with seventeen diplomas on your wall,
a science at the tip of each finger, five languages at
the tip of your tongue, and an extra helping of ambition
between your ears, you can expect fate to present you with
a fat slice of the good life on a silver platter — that's com-
monplace. But if your only diploma is from reform school,
you have nothing at the tips of your fingers but your prints,
no language but what you were born with, and your only
ambition is to be unemployed — and you still haven't given
up the idea of getting rich . . . there's something grandiose
in that. To face Lady Luck like a cross between a pan-
handler and a freedom fighter, to hold out your hand when
you haven't a leg to stand on, that is noble gall, an enviable
itch. I appreciate myself — and why not? Appreciation
should always begin with what's closest to your heart, and
that's yourself. I'm a generous man, I'll give myself away in
marriage. It's going to be a marriage of convenience, but
love enters into it. My girl finds it convenient to love me,
and I love the convenience of her 30,000 thalers. Of course,
money is the root of all evil, but every man has the moral
responsibility to uproot evil wherever he finds it. That's a
piece of wisdom I'll hold under my pet's nose like smelling
salts if she'll faint at the news that I have liberated her from

her evil cash. But I must not spend her golden eggs before I catch my goose. (*Notices Innkeeper entering through the center.*) Uh, uh . . . trouble!

Scene 6

INNKEEPER: Baron . . .

MOON: Yes — what is it?

INNKEEPER: May I respectfully present the bill . . . It's over-due.

MOON: I was just about to take my constitutional. What kind of innkeeper are you, preventing your guest from working up an appetite?

INNKEEPER: Oh, I've no complaints about your appetite . . .

MOON: Without my constitutional I can't bring a morsel to my lips. I'd eat no more than a canary.

INNKEEPER: Well, Mr. Canary, I'm not worried about your lips but your bill.

MOON: All right. How much is that wretched, miserable bill?

INNKEEPER: It's 286 wretched thalers and 36 miserable groschen. I wouldn't have mentioned it except that I have never seen Your Honor toss even the smallest coin to Jepp.

MOON: There's good reason for your observation, my good man. Truth will out and I might as well give it to you straight. The reason why I haven't tossed a coin is that I don't have any.

INNKEEPER: Are you serious?

MOON: I can prove it. Look in my pockets.

INNKEEPER: That's what I get for listening to my wife. She trusts everyone. And you, pauper without a coin, have had the nerve to feed like a prince?

MOON: Only to protect your reputation. You wouldn't want people to say that this is a chophouse that caters to tramps? An inn's reputation is as delicate as a virgin's — but with a difference: an inn becomes suspect if men are asked to leave, and a virgin if they are asked to stay.

INNKEEPER: Fiddle-faddle! No customer of mine leaves here until he's paid up.

MOON: It's a deal. Then I'm provided for life.

INNKEEPER: Enough horseplay! In the end it will turn out that you're not even a baron?

MOON: It turned out that way from the beginning.

INNKEEPER: Well — of all the gall!

MOON: Are *you* a baron? How dare you demand of someone else what you yourself can't offer?

INNKEEPER: But you said . . .

MOON: Of course I said. If you could become a baron by just saying so, the whole world would be an aristocracy.

INNKEEPER: Then your name isn't Moonbeam?

MOON: No, my name is Moon, plain and simple. I added the beam only to support a roof over my head.

INNKEEPER: Do you realize that I can have you arrested?

MOON: You wouldn't do that to a man who, in a way, is your own flesh and blood?

INNKEEPER: You wouldn't claim to be a relative of mine?

MOON: Circumstances leave me no choice. Can you think back thirty years?

INNKEEPER: I have a splendid memory. You can't fool me.

MOON: Of course. Looking back thirty years is nothing for a man who's a hundred years behind his time. You will remember that your father had a waitress by the name of Nina Moon thirty years ago?

INNKEEPER: As if it were only twenty-nine years ago.

MOON: All right. Your mother promised this Nina Moon that if she'd marry and have a baby girl, your mother would be the child's godmother. Well, Nina did marry, sort of, and I happen to be her son, and not her daughter, but that's not my fault. If she'd told me how important it was in time, I might have arranged it. But still, nothing shall prevent me from honoring your mother — God bless her! — as my godmother.

INNKEEPER: Well, that's stretching your kinship a bit far. Is your mother alive?

MOON: She is in the same place my godmother is, the two of them look down on us, and the same thought floats through their celestial minds: "It's a disgrace how that innkeeper bullies our poor little son!"

INNKEEPER: Fishfeathers! Who was your father?

MOON: Pride in ancestry isn't one of my sins. I've never traced my family tree that far back.

INNKEEPER: In short, you can't pay, and there's no hope that someone else will pay for you. So it's jail after all!

MOON: Hold it. You have a curious manner of worming your way into my confidence. The hope that someone else will pay for me borders on certainty.

INNKEEPER: Who'd be stupid enough to pay your bill?

MOON: A woman. Has it escaped you how extremely handsome I am?

INNKEEPER: It has indeed.

MOON: Well, the main thing is that a certain party finds me irresistible.

INNKEEPER: You're engaged?

MOON: Since the last carnival. There I met the unsuspecting sponsor of my economic recovery plans. I was an unemployed servant then, after having been a jobless valet for quite a while.

INNKEEPER: And who is the lucky bride?

MOON: The sister-in-law of Mr. Lard.

INNKEEPER: What? Lucia Thistle? They say she's worth 30,000 thalers!

MOON: Yes, I'm the donkey who likes the Thistle. She came to visit her brother-in-law, I followed her, and that's the reason why you're lucky enough to have me as a guest in your inn.

INNKEEPER: That's one piece of luck I could've done without.

MOON: Well, if you don't see how lucky you are to get a 300-thaler share from my 30,000-thaler dowry, then you're even dumber than they say.

INNKEEPER: Than who says?

MOON: We all have our friends. Keep my mouth full and yours closed, and our worries are over.

INNKEEPER: I wish mine were. Yours I don't care about unless you're worried about my bill. But I'll keep an eye on you. You try to get away from here and I'll stick the coppers on you.

(Exits.)

Scene 7

MOON *(alone)*:   My romance with Lucia needs a shot in the arm. These walks down the garden path don't get me anywhere if they don't lead up the aisle. She loves me but she has money, so you can't expect the kind of octopus clutch you get from a penniless creature when a man has mentioned matrimony. And Lard, having even more money, will be more suspicious still — yet, I'll have to meet him.

(Ferdinand enters without noticing Moon.)

MOON *(watching Ferdinand)*:   Dear me, in what folder of my memory have I filed that face?

FERDINAND *(to himself)*:   I'll simply go to Mr. Lard.

MOON *(to himself)*:   That's what I'll have to do, too.

FERDINAND *(to himself)*:   Alfred made me unsure — is the world really like this . . . do you no longer count when you've lost your money? That would be a nasty world, and my Fritzi is part of the world — she's my entire world. No, she's more, she's my heaven, and heaven ought to be kinder than the world . . .

MOON (*to himself*): That's one of my former employers! (*Loud*) Sir . . .

FERDINAND: Yes?

MOON: Don't you recognize me? Your former valet Moon?

FERDINAND: Oh yes, the good-for-nothing I dismissed last year.

MOON: At your service, again, if you please.

FERDINAND: I wish I could hire someone — even you. To come to Lard with any kind of a servant would help. But I haven't any money to pay you.

MOON: Money has always played a negligible part in my life. I don't need any pay, I simply want to go to the Lard mansion to be near the woman I love.

FERDINAND: You, too? That Lard must collect women as he collects money.

MOON: The two often go together. Don't you see — I serve you, and you serve me. A master without a valet looks shabby in a mansion, and a valet without a master can't even get in the front door. But together we can't lose: Lard will invite you to stay, I'll stay, too, we get free room and board, and a gamble at our respective beloveds.

FERDINAND: Hum — it might work.

MOON: It's the solution to man's economic crisis: if the rich wouldn't always invite other rich people, but the poor — why, everyone would have enough to eat.

FERDINAND: Then all we need is a servant's uniform.

MOON: That we'll fix, presto. (*Takes off his blue coat.*) A couple of weeks ago I was collared by a copper, and that revealed that my collar is lined with yellow, so by ripping it off (*Does it with a knife.*) it makes this coat look like a servant's livery. And, excuse me, Sir, your cap . . . (*Rips some gold braid from Ferdinand's cap and attaches it to his shoulders.*) The master dressed with dignified simplicity, the servant spruced up like a Christmas tree — this must impress any *nouveau riche* ex-butcher.

Scene 8

INNKEEPER (*entering, to Ferdinand*):   Your room is ready . . . (*Noticing the change in Moon's dress*)   What's that?
FERDINAND: My servant, who'll accompany me.
MOON (*softly, to Innkeeper*):   Quiet, that's part of my 30,000-thaler plan.
FERDINAND (*to Innkeeper*):   I don't need any room, thanks. (*Softly, to Moon*)   I've only one silver thaler left.
MOON (*softly, to Ferdinand*):   Toss it to him.
FERDINAND (*to Innkeeper*):   Here's for your trouble. (*Hands him the thaler.*)
INNKEEPER (*bowing and scraping*):   Thank you, Sir.
MOON (*to Ferdinand*):   Here we stand, two Columbuses, who have burned their ships behind them. A new world lies before us — the hearts and the cash of our sweethearts are the America we are to conquer.

(*Moon and Ferdinand leave.*)

INNKEEPER: Well, that's odd. One of them eats nothing and pays well, the other eats well and pays nothing. Most suspicious! Most suspicious!

Scene 9

(*An elegant room in Lard's mansion. Two center and two side doors.*)

LARD: Leave me alone, Lucia, I tell you. Don't fill my head with your fuss and feathers.

LUCIA: Well, it has to be filled with *some*thing!

LARD: Since my wife passed away, I'm used to peace and quiet.

LUCIA: It won't stay quiet with me around. Not as long as you forbid your gardener to let me have the garden key! What will people think?

LARD: They'll think much worse if I let you have the key. (*Looking at her sharply*) Who's that pest who plucks the guitar under your window and howls like a locked-up poodle?

LUCIA (*coquettish*): That's my admirer serenading me. I've kindled a flame in his heart.

LARD: And I'll pour water on his head.

LUCIA (*sighing*): Oh, he is such a dashing young man!

LARD: He would be dashing even faster if I'd pour the water on him. Listen, Lucia — what counts in a husband is wealth, not appearance.

LUCIA: I prefer appearance — and the sooner the better.

LARD: Things have changed, Lucia: you used to be the sister-in-law of a butcher but now you're a scion of a distinguished family of stockholders. A butcher girl can display her wares, but a stockholder's kin must keep hers in a safe deposit box. Our former situation and the present one — that's just like comparing a half pound of tripe to a roast of venison!

LUCIA: My admirer is a gentleman!

LARD: Baloney!

LUCIA: That's *your* meat. But keep your meat cleaver out of my affairs. Once I'm twenty-one . . .

LARD: Once? You're twenty-one twice over, my dear, and that's why you ought to be an example to my daughter. But what my daughter can learn from you is not what I want my daughter to learn. A young girl spoils faster than an unsold fish.

LUCIA: But you forget, my dear brother-in-law, that I'm one goldfish who has not even been caught yet.

LARD: What will the servants think? It's scandalous what goes on under your window.

LUCIA: You have no feelings for tender emotions!

LARD: We are a high-class family now, and that's no place for emotions.

Scene 10

FRITZI (*entering with Ulrike through the center right*): Papa! Papa! Good news. Guess who just arrived?

LARD: Who?

FRITZI: Ferdinand! My Ferdinand!

LARD: What? Büchner? That son-of-a-flop? We'll get rid of *that* admirer in a hurry!

FRITZI: Papa, haven't I always been your obedient daughter?

LARD: Why, yes.

FRITZI: Haven't I always followed your orders?

LARD: Of course.

FRITZI: So you won't doubt my obedience in the future?

LARD: I'd hope not.

FRITZI: Well — there's one sure way to keep a daughter obedient: don't order her to do things she doesn't want to do.

LARD: I won't give *you* any order, Fritzi, but to him I'll say, "Go on, move!"

FRITZI: That's all right. Build us a home and tell us, "move," and we'll move the next day.

LARD (*angrily*): What? You'd dare?

FRITZI: Don't get angry, Papa. But I'll never marry anyone but Ferdinand because I love him.

LARD: That's no reason to get married. A bride can profit from love only if it comes from her father — provided he's rich.

LUCIA: So you love her and will give her your cash and blessing.

LARD: No. I said no such thing.

LUCIA: I never saw such a sausage mind — tightly stuffed but no one knows with what.

ULRIKE: Please try and see it Fritzi's way, Uncle Lard. Ferdinand loved her before his luck changed . . .

LARD: His luck and my mind, both. A rich father can't give away his daughter to a pauper, it's against the law of economics. (*To Ulrike*) And I'll have a word with you, too, about love.

ULRIKE: With me?

LARD: You dared fall in love with my secretary, Alfred, without my permission?

ULRIKE (*embarrassed*): I am . . . I have . . .

LARD: You have very little money, he has a very small salary —

ULRIKE: But we want to get married.

LARD: Then ask my permission. Love is revolting, and poverty even more so. No one should be made to suffer from both. There isn't much you can do about poverty, but you can get rid of love quickly when you are poor and get married.

ULRIKE: Then we have hope?

LARD: The faster the better. Marriage yes, love no.

SERVANT (*entering through the center*): Herr Ferdinand Buchner wishes to pay his respects . . .

LARD: Well, if that's all he can pay, let him wait . . .

FRITZI: No, Papa, that isn't high class to humble a man who once . . .

LARD: You're right. (*To servant*) Show him in. I'll make

him eat humble pie by serving him pheasant on a silver platter. With noble irony I'll display him my riches, so that knowing he's broke will break him twice as hard and he won't dare even to think about matrimony.

Scene 11

(*Ferdinand enters from left with Moon, who is carrying Ferdinand's little suitcase.*)

FERDINAND: My dear Lard, I'm so glad about your good fortune.

LARD: Herr *von* Lard, if you please . . .

MOON (*respectfully approaching Lard*): Is a simple servant permitted to kiss this illustrious hand?

LARD (*smiling, holding out his hand*): Help yourself.

MOON: A highly interesting hand, this: five sausage fingers that have learned to handle cold cash as deftly as they used to handle hot dogs. Yes, "tempus mutampus," which is Latin for "From smoking hams to smoking Havanas."

LARD (*to himself*): A charming fellow.

FERDINAND (*has meanwhile greeted Fritzi*): So you thought of me sometimes during my absence?

FRITZI: Only one time, for I've never stopped thinking of you.

MOON (*to himself*): This joke has been cracked often, but it's still waterproof and unsinkable.

LARD (*stepping between the lovers, to Ferdinand*): You wanted to pay your respects to *me*!

FERDINAND: And also to . . .

LARD: Quiet. Pay your respects here (*Pointing at himself*)

and pay your last visit there (*Pointing at Fritzi*) and
these will be the last two installments you owe us.

FERDINAND: But, Sir, I have . . .

LARD: You have nothing, that's the point. You're a down-
and-out have-nothing!

MOON (*to Lard*): Excuse me, Sir, but that's what *you* are!

LARD: What? How dare you . . . ?

MOON: You took *down* your apron, you are *out* of your
butcher shop, and you *have nothing* to fear of the future!

LARD (*to Ferdinand*): I like your servant. I'll hire him from
you. You and a servant, that's silly anyway. Just like a
family with no money for food, and keeping an expensive
dog.

FERDINAND: I know you want to hurt my feelings, Herr von
Lard, but . . .

LARD: Feelings! A poor man can't afford any feelings except
hunger, and we'll take care of that today. You'll stay for
dinner and have your fill.

FERDINAND: No, that's too much, I'll . . .

ULRIKE (*to Fritzi*): Try and calm him.

FRITZI (*to Ferdinand*): Please bear it for my sake!

LARD (*to Fritzi and Ulrike*): What's all this whispering?
There's the fermez-la-porte. Understand?

FRITZI: Papa, don't drive your obedient daughter to desperation!

LARD: No. I'll just drive you to your room.

ULRIKE: Come, Fritzi, let's go. (*Exits with Fritzi through
left center.*)

LARD (*to Ferdinand*): I'll call my secretary. He can drag
you around, I can't be bothered. (*Exits through left center.*)

FERDINAND: Oh, Fritzi! Only for you I'm willing to bear
this!

(*Exits through center.*)

Scene 12

MOON (*alone*):   As the Greek philosopher said, "Between being invited and being invited is as much difference as between a kiss and a slap." The way one is asked for dinner is a magic spell which can change a rice pudding into a sacher torte, but it also can turn a Wiener schnitzel into a blood sausage. What will my master wear for dinner? (*Opens the suitcase.*) A spencer, a waistcoat, trousers — not much! A man wouldn't believe what a man needs to look like a man. It's odd how a man, creation's masterpiece, has to spend himself poor just to cover up the masterpiece. (*Takes a brush from the suitcase and brushes the suit.*)

LUCIA (*from the left*):   Well, what is the meaning of *this*?

MOON: Lucia!

LUCIA: Baron Moonbeam! What are you doing?

MOON: You're surprised because I'm brushing a suit — what would you say if you saw me shine shoes?

LUCIA: Such disguise?

MOON: For the sake of love!

LUCIA: But as a servant!

MOON: For love no disguise is too low if it serves the purpose. Jupiter set an example for all lovers when he disguised himself as a bull to win Europa, and ever since then, bull has proved effective to win a girl's heart.

LUCIA: Do you know, my Greek god, how long it's been since we saw each other last?

MOON: Three days . . . that's 72 hours, or . . . let me figure it out . . . (*Scribbles on his cuff*) . . . 4,320 minutes, or . . . 259,200 seconds. Since the heart beats three times each second, and my heart beats only for you, it beat . . . wait a minute . . . 388,800 times for nothing because you weren't with me.

LUCIA: I wish we could be together, always.

MOON: That can be arranged. Let me catch you, my turtle-dove.

LUCIA: Are you proposing?

MOON: Yes, I am proposing, my golden-eyed bobolink. Let's collect bits of straw and build a resting place for your nest eggs.

LUCIA (*nestling against him*): Darling!

MOON: Every morning I'll be up to catch the first worm — just for you!

LUCIA (*nestling*): Oh, you are so romantic!

MOON: We'll live in the clouds, and every winter we'll migrate to Italy.

LUCIA: Wherever you say.

MOON: But coming down to earth for a moment, do you mind, my pigeon, if I bring up a ticklish subject?

LUCIA: Tickle away, my dear woodpecker.

MOON: You know of course, my little goose, that it's not your golden eggs I'm after. Nevertheless, I have to make certain that I can feather our nest in the manner to which you are accustomed. In a moment of truth, second only to the present, I've confided in you that I'm of a noble breed, and that breeds trouble for a bride. My father has his nose up in the air and soon he will sniff the smoked ham of the ex-butcher. Prejudice, you know, runs strong in blue blood.

LUCIAS What are you leading up to?

MOON: The aisle, I hope. But you know that to marry below rank is always risky, for a father may turn off the liquid assets. But what do I care about my own money? It's the least of my worries, believe me. But I'm all the more concerned about yours. According to folklore, you're worth 30,000 thalers.

LUCIA: You're off 10,000.

MOON: How folks always overstate the truth!

LUCIA: Now you're off 20,000. I'm worth 40,000!
MOON: How folks always understate the truth! So your figure is fortyish!
LUCIA: Forty thousandish.
MOON: Oh, you bird of paradise, you sweet woman of forty! Please forgive my excursion from the romantic into the financial . . .

Scene 13

(*Lard enters through the center, unnoticed by Moon and Lucia.*)

MOON (*continuing*):   . . . but you see, it's a delicate situation if one is of noble birth.
LARD (*to himself*):   Noble birth? Is he really . . . ?
LUCIA: Don't worry, we won't starve even if your blue-blooded papa turns off the supply line.
LARD (*to himself*):   Blue-blooded papa? No doubt, he is . . .
LUCIA (*noticing Lard, to Moon*):   A plague upon him, he heard . . .
MOON: Who dares . . . ? (*Sees Lard, bows respectfully*) Oh, I beg your pardon.
LARD (*to himself*):   There, the nobleman's slip is showing. (*Aloud to Lucia*) Sister-in-law, go to your room!
LUCIA: Go jump in the Danube!
LARD: I said, go. This calls for a few words between me and him and the bedpost.

(*Lucia exits grumbling at side door left.*)

Scene 14

LARD (*approaches Moon, importantly*):   Baron . . .
MOON: But, Sir . . .

LARD: Nonsense. Shake! One nobleman to another!

MOON: Then you . . .

LARD: . . . know that you're one of us. I have an eye for such things.

MOON: The unerring instinct of the true nobleman spotting another.

LARD: But why the disguise?

MOON: I want to be loved for myself, not for my title or my money.

LARD: Is everybody in love around here? I hate love, it's so low-class.

MOON: Yes, if one considers (*Contemptuously*) the type of people who often fall in love I'd be inclined to agree with you. But on the other hand if one considers (*Nose in air*) the type of people who often fall in love, then I can't share your opinion. That much is certain: secret love is always noble, but displaying emotions — that's plebeian. So you see — it all depends. Or, to put it in familiar terms: love is like hash — you have to have confidence to enjoy it.

LARD: You talk like a man who has been in love before.

MOON: Not seriously but often.

LARD: May I ask your name?

MOON: The real one I don't care to give, and a false one is of no use to you.

LARD (*impressed*): And Your Excellency wishes to marry my sister-in-law?

MOON: The sooner the better.

LARD: That's what I told my secretary, too. The best thing is to get it over with quickly. He'll marry Cousin Ulrike tomorrow. You can get married tomorrow, too.

MOON: Oh, blissful day!

LARD: That is, tomorrow evening.

MOON: Oh, blissful evening! A few hours make no difference.

LARD: But I demand a favor in return.

MOON: Granted.

LARD: I have a daughter —

MOON: You want me to marry her, too?

LARD (*wagging a finger at him*):   Baron, you're a wag. She's in love —

MOON: With whom?

LARD: With a lowly person, with your master. That is . . .

MOON: That is, with that seamy character who seems to be my master and whose valet I seem to be.

LARD: Right! And I'd like to louse up that romance.

MOON: I'll louse it up for you.

LARD: It won't be so easy.

MOON: Oh, I'm an expert louse. I'll find a way. But my master must not know who I am.

LARD: I don't know that myself.

MOON: Good. Discretion! I must be surrounded by an ocean of discretion.

LARD (*shouting*):   From me, no one will ever learn that you are really a . . .

MOON (*holds his hand over Lard's mouth*):   Shush!

Scene 15

SERVANT (*entering through the center left*):   The innkeeper of the Silver Stallion is outside.

LARD: The Innkeeper?

MOON: The Innkeeper! Herr von Lard, a man in your position won't stoop so low as to receive a miserable innkeeper personally?

LARD: That's true, why should I expose myself to his vulgar presence? (*To servant*)   Ask him what he wants.

SERVANT: He says he has an important disclosure to make.
LARD: A disclosure! Send him in.

(Servant exits through the center.)

MOON: I have to rush off to tell Lucia about the wedding. But before I go I must warn you.
LARD: About what?
MOON (*mysteriously*): About the Innkeeper. He's a name-dropper. He always claims he knows everybody. He may say he knows *me*.
LARD: That blabber!
MOON: Well, anyway, don't believe him. He may even tell you that I'm not what I appear to be. I told you that myself.

(Exits.)

Scene 16

INNKEEPER (*entering through the center right and looking after Moon*): Aha!
LARD: What kind of manners are these — to say "Aha!" when you enter a room?
INNKEEPER: Beg your pardon, Sir. I didn't mean you.
LARD: You'd better not say "Aha!" to me. A dumb word, that, but many people have a silly way of saying "Aha!" at every opportunity.
INNKEEPER: What I meant to say is that there is a certain party who hasn't paid his bill.
LARD: Aha!
INNKEEPER: And the bill amounts to 286 thalers and 36 groschen.
LARD: Aha!

INNKEEPER: And the party in question had the nerve to set foot in your mansion.

LARD: Aha!

INNKEEPER: Now you see, Sir, you're saying "Aha!" yourself.

LARD: Oaf! How dare you put words in my mouth!

INNKEEPER: No, no, Sir, I wouldn't dream of it.

LARD: All right. What is that disclosure you have to make?

INNKEEPER: Today two men came to visit your mansion.

LARD: I know that.

INNKEEPER: One of them is more than he appears.

LARD: I know that, too.

INNKEEPER: And the other is less than he appears to be.

LARD: I know all that. Is that all you have to tell me?

INNKEEPER: No. One of them has designs on your sister-in-law.

LARD: That's old stuff.

INNKEEPER: Yes, but . . .

LARD: What else do you want, worm?

INNKEEPER: I want your permission, Sir, to bring up a copper to arrest the impostor for not paying his bill.

LARD: By all means, friend, do that. (*To himself*) That solves everything. It gets rid of that pauper, Buchner, and saves the Baron the trouble of thinking up a scheme to wreck Fritzi's romance! (*To Innkeeper*) Go ahead! Arrest! The sooner the better. (*Exits.*)

INNKEEPER (*calling after him*):   I'll be back with a copper! (*To himself*) And then, Moon, you'll be mine down to your last quarter!

(*Exits through the center.*)

Scene 17

(*Ulrike enters through center right, talking to Alfred, Ferdinand, and Fritzi.*)

ULRIKE (*to Alfred*): You don't seem to be very happy that Herr von Lard wants us to get married tomorrow?

ALFRED: How can you doubt it . . . ?

FERDINAND (*to Fritzi*): They can get married, but for us there's no hope . . .

FRITZI: Don't worry — Papa is a little stubborn, but I'm so obedient that he'll do what I want.

ULRIKE (*to Alfred*): I have no parents to ask for permission, and you, too, are independent in your decisions. So we can get married tomorrow.

ALFRED (*hesitantly*): Yes.

ULRIKE: There's something you are hiding from me.

ALFRED: Well, I do have a friend — a relative, in fact — whom I want to tell about us.

ULRIKE: You want him to be present at our wedding?

ALFRED (*eagerly*): Yes, yes, that's it — I think I should go to Vienna and invite him.

ULRIKE: Alfred, you're not holding back something?

ALFRED: No, Ulrike, certainly not.

FERDINAND (*to Alfred*): But Lard has already made the arrangements . . .

Scene 18

LARD (*entering from left*): All right, Alfred, Ulrike, the priest is notified for tomorrow, and the notary is in the next room to draft what's needed. Grooms always need to be drafted. (*Laughs, self-satisfied.*) Pretty good, eh? Well, you lucky couple . . . (*Points to the door, right.*)

ALFRED (*after a short hesitation*): As you say, Sir. (*Guides Ulrike to the side door, right.*)

ULRIKE (*worried at Alfred's strange behavior*): Alfred . . .

SERVANT (*entering, to Lard*): A letter, Sir.

LARD (*taking the letter*): From where?

SERVANT: From Vienna.

LARD: Sealed with a signet ring!

FERDINAND: That's a coat of arms!

LARD (*breaks open the letter, to Alfred*): Secretary, read me these here scratchings! (*Hands him the letter.*)

ALFRED (*taking the letter to Ferdinand*): Heavens, from my father!

ULRIKE (*watching Alfred, whispering to Fritzi*): He's upset. What do you think is the matter?

LARD: Women leave the room on such occasions . . .

FRITZI (*softly to Ferdinand*): You tell me later what was in that letter!

LARD (*continuing*): . . . and don't return until they're called. (*Sharply to Fritzi*) Understand?

FRITZI (*angrily*): All right, all right. You know I'm your obedient daughter.

(*Exits with Ulrike, who keeps looking worriedly at Alfred, through the center right.*)

Scene 19

LARD: Now from whom is this letter?

ALFRED: It's signed by the Marquis François Vincelli.

LARD: What, the millionaire who buys properties like others buy eggs? Read, Secretary, read!

ALFRED (*reads*): "Sir! An incredible rumor has come to my ears . . . about my son staying at your home, where he is said to be paying court to one of the females in your family . . ."

LARD (*amazed, to himself*): So that's who Mr. Incognito is!

Quite a catch for that Thistle in her wilted condition.
(*To Alfred*)   Don't just stand there. Read!

ALFRED (*continuing the letter*): "As you must realize the
absurdity of any expectation you may have as to my assent
to such a humiliation for the house of Vincelli —"

LARD: Humiliation? Just because he inherited his castle,
and I had to buy mine? Or because his family has had
their noses up for centuries, and I'm still practicing?

ALFRED (*continuing*): "I count on your cooperation to put
an immediate stop to such foolishness, if these rumors
should be true at all. I'll come and convince myself . . ."
(*To Ferdinand*)   Heavens, he's coming here!

LARD: Go on, go on!

ALFRED (*continuing*): "You can expect me within an hour
after receipt of this letter. Meanwhile I will thank you to
observe the strictest secrecy vis-à-vis my son. Signed, Marquis Vincelli."

FERDINAND (*softly to Alfred*): Good Lord, what are you
going to do now?

LARD (*walking up and down, smiling*): He is coming in
person, that's good. He doesn't expect such elegance, such
class. Just wait, old uppercrust. I'll dazzle you with a crust
of my own. I'll wine and dine you with all the groceries
that money can buy. But no sausages.

ALFRED (*to Ferdinand*): I've got to talk to Father, confess
all, and beg his forgiveness.

LARD (*to Ferdinand*): You've stomach luck today. A dinner
like that will fill you up for days . . .

FERDINAND (*indignant*): Allow me . . .

LARD: Yes, I'll allow you to sit at the table with us but
don't carry on too much. I'd rather wrap a bottle for you
tomorrow when you get on your way. (*To Alfred*) Secretary! You must go and meet our guest. Don't let him stay
at the Silver Stallion. Bring him up here to the mansion.

ALFRED: Yes, Sir.

FERDINAND (*to Alfred*): I'll go with you.

> (*Both leave through center left.*)

Scene 20

LARD: I'll have to tell the notary to come back tomorrow. Today there are more important things to do than draw up wedding contracts. (*Opens the door right and calls in*) Hullo, there, fellow . . . (*Continues to talk into the other room.*)

MOON (*enters anxiously from the left*): I saw coppers . . . if they're after me . . . if that innkeeper is mean enough . . .

LARD (*turns and sees Moon*): Dear Baron . . . a little problem has come up . . . will you do me a favor and hide for a while?

MOON: Oh, with the greatest of pleasure!

LARD: There are reasons.

MOON (*looking toward the window*): I can plainly see them.

LARD: You go to the left wing of the mansion . . .

MOON: One wing is as good as another. (*To himself*) I wish I had two. (*To Lard*) Let's go, I'm flying!

LARD: It's not that urgent.

MOON: I don't know why you want to hide me, but it's all right with me.

LARD: All right, this way then. (*Directs him toward the center left.*)

MOON: No, no, not through here. We might run into someone.

LARD: If you wish, we can also . . . (*Points at center right.*)

MOON: Yes, that's better.

LARD: I'm delighted that you are so cooperative. One can see that you have breeding! (*Embraces him.*)

Scene 21

(*Innkeeper enters through center left with two policemen.*)

INNKEEPER: Grab him! (*Pointing at Moon*) That's the one!

POLICEMEN (*approaching Moon*): You come with us!

LARD: What? Are you fellows drunk?

INNKEEPER (*to Lard*): That's the one who . . .

LARD: Innkeeper, I'll make mincemeat of you!

INNKEEPER: But my 286 thalers and 36 groschen . . .

LARD: If this gentleman hasn't paid, he must know why.

MOON: I certainly do.

LARD (*to Moon*): These are the fine points the rabble can't get into their noddle. (*To the policemen*) Come over here. (*Leads them to the foreground and whispers, pointing at Moon*) This gentleman is a — I'm not at liberty to say what — but he is — (*Indicates that he is something high and whispers into the ears of the policemen*) That jabbernowle there doesn't know this. (*Points at the Innkeeper.*)

POLICEMEN: Well, in that case . . . (*Take off their caps and bow before Moon.*)

INNKEEPER (*to policemen*): What are you doing? That's the one . . .

LARD (*to Innkeeper*): Shut up! (*Rings a bell.*)

INNKEEPER: But I assure you, Sir . . . (*Four servants enter from the center left.*)

LARD: Servants, throw this ruffian out! (*Points at Innkeeper.*)

INNKEEPER: But you agreed that I . . .

LARD (*to Moon*): I owe you that satisfaction!

MOON (*grandly*): Oh, let him go . . . I don't like to cause a scene . . .

LARD: No, no. Without a good bounce the whole thing has no snap.

INNKEEPER: But . . .
LARD (*to servants*):   Go to it!
SERVANTS: Out you go!

(*Lively music. Servants shove the struggling Innkeeper out the door. Policemen laugh. Lard embraces Moon.*)

CURTAIN

ACT TWO

(Dining room in the Silver Stallion Inn)

Scene 1

WIFE OF INNKEEPER: Good heavens! Such a guest and my husband is out!
WAITER: Four horses and a carriage!
WIFE: A private coach!
WAITER: A manservant, a coachman, and a groom!
WIFE: Hurry, hurry! They're coming!

Scene 2

VINCELLI *(in traveling outfit, to his servants)*:   Put everything down here. Where is the hotelier?
WIFE OF INNKEEPER *(with a deep curtsy)*:   Beg your pardon, Your Excellency, we don't have any guests right now. We had one, but his name wasn't Hot-el-yay.
VINCELLI: Imbecile — I mean the innkeeper.
WIFE: I beg your pardon. My husband will be back any moment.
VINCELLI *(to servants)*:   Depart! *(To Innkeeper's wife)* Madame, a word with you.

(All servants leave.)

Scene 3

WIFE OF INNKEEPER: At your service, Your Excellency.

VINCELLI: Tell me, my good woman, is there in this village a certain — Florian Lard, I believe, is his name.

WIFE: Yes, his mansion is out there, he's our lord and master . . .

VINCELLI (*angrily*): Mansion — lord and master — revolting! A former sausage stuffer! Ugh! What kind of a person is this . . . Lard-Lord?

WIFE (*ingratiatingly*): Nothing, Your Excellency, nothing, really. If it pleases Your Excellency, he's just an ordinary person without rank.

VINCELLI: Have you heard — it's an absurd rumor — something about a liaison between a young man from the city and a — a female relative of this porkmonger?

WIFE: Well, my husband did say . . .

VINCELLI: Exactly what?

WIFE: There is talk of an elopement.

VINCELLI (*irritated*): Elopement!

WIFE: With Your Excellency's permission, yes.

VINCELLI: With my permission! Oh you . . . just wait . . . ! (*To Innkeeper's wife*) The young man in question is staying at the . . . uh . . . mansion of this . . . uh . . . Lard?

WIFE: He is now, I believe, but up to yesterday he stayed here, in this inn, and he still owes us 286 thalers and 36 groschen.

VINCELLI: No matter! Oh, if this were the worst! I suppose he uses a false name?

WIFE: Oh, it must be the falsest name in the world. (*Suppressing a sigh*) He's full of falsehood, this Moon!

VINCELLI: Send me one of my servants!

WIFE: Right away, Your Excellency.

(*She exits through center.*)

Scene 4

VINCELLI: It's true! Wretched truth, outrage, blight of my family tree! How fortunate that I've come in time. Even if it should cost me half my fortune . . .

KLING (*coming through center, pointing back*): Your Excellency, your son . . .

VINCELLI (*amazed*): What? He . . . here, the reprobate? I don't want to see him now . . . tell him that! Tell him to wait for me here, to prepare himself for the thunderbolt that will strike his head. But first I want to talk to this . . . this family of wurst peddlers! (*Exits through side right.*)

KLING: Here he is!

Scene 5

ALFRED (*entering through the center*): Wasn't that my father leaving here?

KLING: In the foulest of moods. Oh, Master Alfred, in what adventures are you mixed up?

ALFRED: In only one, old friend, the most beautiful of all, a love adventure which is going to be the adventure of my life, my happiness. I must talk to Father right away . . .

KLING: I wouldn't advise that, Master Alfred. I know the Marquis. Wait till he sends for you.

ALFRED: You're right . . . (*Reflecting*) You know, my dear Kling, you have been with Father for so many years . . . you have his ear . . . you must talk to him. Didn't you tell me that Father himself, when he was very young, was in love with a commoner?

KLING: He doesn't want to be reminded of that.

ALFRED: You must do it for me!

KLING: How will that help? Your father sacrificed his youth-
ful romance and married the bride his father chose for him.
ALFRED: Has Father been happy?
KLING: He never speaks of it.
ALFRED: Where is he now?
KLING: He's getting ready to go up to the mansion.
ALFRED: Then I have hope. He will see my Ulrike. Meet-
ing Lard will be a shock to him but the contrast will be
all the more dramatic when he sees my angel — (*A bell
rings in the room to the right.*)
KLING: Ah, the Marquis — I must go in.
ALFRED: I'll wait for Father here.

(*Kling   exits   right,   Alfred   left.*)

Scene 6

(*Room in Lard's mansion. In the back an arch,
right and left doors, in the right foreground a
window.*)

MOON (*entering from the left*):   I'm not under lock and key
but it's so dull here that I see little difference between
being hidden and being locked up. The three-quarters of
an hour I've been here seem like a week. Solitary confine-
ment is not my type of vacation. A year of that must give
eternity a good run for its money. And I don't even know
why Lard is hiding me. Nor from whom. (*Picks up a
guitar from the table.*) Good thing I have my guitar with
me — let's see, I have to get my bearings. This is the left
wing, so over there must be the right drumstick, and there's
Lucia's window. I'll let her know where I am. (*Opens the*

window and sits down on the window sill.) Being an artist comes in handy. (*Plucks the same two chords on the guitar, repetitively.*)

Scene 7

FERDINAND (*entering through the arch*): Ah, here you are. I've been looking for you everywhere.

MOON: Well, think of that. I completely forgot that I'm your valet. You come as if I'd sent for you.

FERDINAND: *You*, sent for *me*?

MOON: Yes, I want to give you two weeks' notice.

FERDINAND: You're only a make-believe valet anyway.

MOON: Well, I'll give you make-believe notice, then. I'm getting married.

FERDINAND: So quickly?

MOON: Yes, the bride, the dowry, Lard's consent, it's all settled!

FERDINAND: Some people have all the luck. Not I — everything goes wrong with me.

MOON: How about becoming *my* valet?

FERDINAND: Now don't be insolent!

MOON: I just meant to be friendly. You were my master, and that brought *me* luck; maybe I can do the same for you.

FERDINAND: I came here full of hope but everything was different from the way I'd expected. Lard has become an insufferable snob!

MOON: A natural consequence of sudden wealth. You may notice a similar change in me today — and just wait till tomorrow!

FERDINAND: But my Fritzi is unchanged — warm, understanding, lovable!

Moon: That's good.

Ferdinand: I have no reason to doubt her.

Moon: That's very good.

Ferdinand: I can't say that she's given me the least occasion . . .

Moon: That's extremely good.

Ferdinand: And yet, I have certain doubts . . .

Moon: That's good, too.

Ferdinand: What do you mean by that?

Moon: Oh, nothing, I'm just in an agreeable mood.

Ferdinand: Are you hinting at something? Is there anything about Fritzi you know?

Moon: I . . . oh, what could I . . . Of course, I might . . . but, as I said before . . . (*Accompanies his words with gestures designed to arouse suspicion.*)

Ferdinand: She appears unchanged, but that may be only appearance.

Moon: Spoken like a man. One must have faith in a woman but never trust her.

Ferdinand: I see you know women. You're right: one must not trust blindly.

Moon: Yet, that's the best way to trust 'em. If you peek, you might see them cheat.

Ferdinand: Not my Fritzi. She'd never cheat!

Moon: No, not Fritzi. She'd pass any test.

Ferdinand: I'd never stoop so low as to test her.

Moon: That's smart. You test a woman and you find she's done her homework well and knows more than you think.

Ferdinand (*with sudden decision*): I'm going to test Fritzi!

Moon (*quickly*): Can I help?

Ferdinand: Yes, you must help me figure out a way. That's the last service I'll ask of you.

Moon: Well, we could . . . if . . . suppose . . . yes, I've got it!

Ferdinand: What is it, Moon? What's your plan?

Moon: You take a walk in the garden. Don't talk to her and be back in an hour.

Ferdinand: How will that help?

Moon (*looking back through the arch*): Here comes Fritzi's maid. Say "Baron" to me so she can hear it!

Ferdinand: I don't understand.

Moon: Here she comes! Say, "Goodbye, my dear Baron!" But loud.

Ferdinand: But how . . . (*Sees Philippina enter through the arch*) Goodbye, my dear Baron!

Moon (*with pointed nonchalance*): *Au revoir!*

Scene 8

Philippina (*surprised*): Either I haven't heard right, or Herr Buchner has gone crazy.

Moon (*haughtily*): How so?

Philippina: He said "Baron" to you.

Moon (*affecting annoyance*): Isn't one ever safe from being overheard by the domestics?

Philippina: You a baron? You can tell that to a nincompoop!

Moon (*proudly*): I've already disclosed it to Herr von Lard.

Philippina: Well, he may swallow it but . . .

Moon: I see my servant's uniform has deceived you. (*With distinguished confidence*) Disguise, *ma petite*, pure disguise!

Philippina: This uniform a disguise? That's just like a parrot saying that he's borrowed his green and red feathers for a masquerade!

Moon: Mademoiselle, you mock me, but as a matter of fact . . .

PHILIPPINA: As a matter of fact, my mistress has sent me to ask you in confidence how Herr Buchner has behaved while he was traveling abroad.

MOON: My old friend Buchner? I met him in Dresden when I left the army . . .

PHILIPPINA: I see. A foot soldier getting the boot . . .

MOON: Foot soldier? Child, I was a major.

PHILIPPINA: A major fibster, yes.

MOON (*irritated*):   Why, you little slut . . . (*Catching himself*) . . . that's what I would call you if I weren't a baron.

PHILIPPINA (*suppressing a snicker*):   Well, you and your good friend Buchner — did you break many Dresden china dolls?

MOON: Tell your mistress that women threw themselves at him but he withstood the bridal waves of temptation like a two-legged Gibraltar . . . are these the words of a valet, or do you now recognize the vocabulary of the noblemen?

PHILIPPINA: Noblesse shows itself in deeds not words.

MOON: I know what you're hinting at, but you're hinting up the wrong family tree. I'm from good stock but, unfortunately, my stocks aren't too good at the moment.

PHILIPPINA: This confession to a maidservant is the best proof of vulgarity.

MOON: Why? It simply proves that I'm not one of those who let their money go to their heads.

PHILIPPINA: At least you'd know where it was.

MOON: My money is imprisoned in the walls of my family chateau. They had so many cracks I had them repaired to keep the draft out when I fell heir to the castle.

PHILIPPINA: Yes, those castles in the air are drafty, especially when occupied by windbags!

MOON: Now the castle is in good shape but I'm in ruins. Impoverished.

PHILIPPINA: An impoverished baron would slip his last thaler to a maid.

MOON: That's what I did to the last one I met. Your rotten luck . . . You're one maid late. Only a rich marriage can fix me up!

PHILIPPINA (*laughing*): "A rich marriage can fix me up." . . . What kind of talk is this? A baron might have said: "Only a golden band of matrimony can restore the brilliance of my ancestral home."

MOON: Don't you see, bondwoman, that I'm trying to talk down to make myself understood by a maid?

PHILIPPINA: A maid has a way of understanding what a baron is trying to tell her, don't you worry!

MOON: Well, anyway, a rich bride has been offered to me.

PHILIPPINA: Oh, I know the kind of brides who offer themselves.

MOON: Impudent! Her father made the offer. In a word, Herr von Lard wants me for a son-in-law.

PHILIPPINA: Miss Fritzi?

MOON: I refused, of course. She's the fiancée of my friend.

PHILIPPINA (*startled and changing her tone*): You are poor and refuse a rich bride to help a friend?

MOON: Not that alone . . . I wouldn't think of living off my wife's money. I'd rather be poor than soil my soul.

PHILIPPINA (*watching him with growing respect*): Now I'm beginning to believe you are one!

MOON: What?

PHILIPPINA: A baron.

MOON (*bows in acknowledgment*): My refusal made Lard furious, but he's angry anyway about Miss Fritzi's stubbornness.

PHILIPPINA: I always tell her to give in to him once in a while.

Moon: You know what? Have Miss Fritzi come over here in an hour. I'll tell her a way to pacify her father and get his permission to marry her Ferdinand Buchner.

Philippina: Would you really . . . ? Baron, I have to apologize . . .

Moon: Never mind.

Philippina (*grumbling to herself, while leaving*): A false baron is harder to spot than a bride in her second month.

(*Exits through the arch, right.*)

Scene 9

Moon (*alone*): Adieu! It's all set! Too bad I told Buchner to come back in an hour. Now I have nothing to do but walk up and down, and I don't like that because it starts me thinking. Most people don't like to get lost in thought because it's unfamiliar territory. But at least I've convinced the maid. She'll send Fritzi. I'm making progress. You can't help making progress . . . it's such a progressive age, this nineteenth century. Every week you read about a new invention. I don't see how people lived before all these things got invented!

Song

1. How opium works
   Was discovered by Turks.
   It helped them forget
   Their blood, tears and sweat.
   In Vienna, the patients
   In big operations
   Smoked opium pipes

To cut out their gripes.
No pain was inflicted,
But now they're addicted,
So that cure didn't last,
It's a thing of the past.

I see by the paper
That sulfurous vapor
Is now used by surgeons
On grandmas and virgins.
They cut off your arm,
It works like a charm.
The dentist has lost
His dread (save for cost),
For sulfurous smoke
Makes the pulling a joke.
So let's celebrate,
For progress is great!

However, they still cut a person apart.
They cut off his hope and they tear out his heart.
And many a man gets to feel the old knife
When he is cut off from his kids and his wife.
A fast operator will bring you much grief —
No vapor of sulfur will give you relief.
At progress I look, and admit:
It ain't, after all, such a hit.

2.   For years now, the mail
     Has been slow as a snail.
     Delivered by buggy
     It was poky and sluggy.
     The news that you told
     In your letter was old.

By the time it was read
You might well have been dead.
And all this did once pass
By the name of "first-class."
And such mail they called fast —
It's a thing of the past.

I'd like now to mention
The latest invention:
They string out a wire,
By electrical fire;
You send out a message
In this new express age.
You can now send by cable
Your passion to Mabel,
Or, as quickly as eighty
Miles per minute, to Katie.
So let's celebrate,
For progress is great!

However — some news you don't need the same day.
A man gets a wire ninety-five miles away:
"Your wife and your best friend are paramours. Stop."
But can he electrically now blow his top?
A telegraph message won't do it — no thanks!
It carries just words but it doesn't send spanks.
At progress I look, and admit:
It ain't, after all, such a hit.

ENCORE

But man did much more —
Invent and explore.
Explorers went forth

To poles, south and north.
Some sweated like crazy
At the River Zambesi
While others would shiver
At a Siberian river.
They mapped with devotion
Every mountain and ocean,
And all had a blast —
But that's a thing of the past.

Now several nations
Do space explorations.
They map out a pattern
To check life on Saturn;
To see if some genus
Developed on Venus;
If people on Jupiter
Perhaps are still stupider.
As a start we will soon
Land a man on the moon.
So let's celebrate —
For progress is great!

However — to find the moon made out of cheese
Will not feed the hungry nor reduce the obese.
To explore its dark side for whatever it's worth
Will not brighten the dark spots we still have on earth.
The man in the moon we will reach long before
We'll get to our fellow men living next door.

Scene 10

(*An elegant room in Lard's mansion. Doors in the center and left.*)

LARD (*entering from the left, to servant*): Go look out the window and make a hell of a racket when you see the carriage. And when he gets off, have everybody dash about like crazy. I'll show him that I have more flunkies than he.

SERVANT: Yes, Sir. (*Exits through the center.*)

LARD: Imagine, a real marquis paying me a visit! And a Bintchelli marrying a Lard! But why does it have to be Lucia? Why not my Fritzi? The girl is pretty . . . I'll dangle her in front of the young marquis' nose . . . and I bet he'll bite. But first we must get rid of Buchner . . . and the young marquis promised to help me . . . he doesn't even know that he is getting rid of his own rival! And meanwhile I have to impress the father!

SERVANT (*calling through the door*): He's coming! He's here! (*Exits again.*)

LARD: Holy liverwurst, I must strike a noble pose. He's got to surprise me reading. George!

SECOND SERVANT (*entering*): Yes, Sir?

LARD: Do we have a book in the house?

(*Second Servant looks around, then goes to a table and removes a book that had supported a short leg. He hands it to Lard.*)

LARD: Good — it's nice and thick. (*Sits down and strikes a pose.*) And now stand at the door and announce him, but loud. Don't mumble — as if announcing a tailor!

SECOND SERVANT: Yes, Sir. (*Opens the middle door and stands under it.*)

LARD: I've got to play it right . . . I'll just do whatever he does, so I can't miss!

SECOND SERVANT (*at the door, announcing*): The Marquis de Vincelli!

LARD: Louder, you ass!

Second Servant (*shouting, almost in Vincelli's ear*): The Marquis de Vincelli!

Scene 11

Vincelli (*entering, to himself*): Clumsy oaf! (*To Lard, with a condescending nod*) Herr Lard, I presume?

Lard (*rising from his chair and imitating Vincelli's nod*): Herr Vincelli, I presume?

Vincelli: Marquis de Vincelli, yes.

Lard: Herr von Lard, yes. (*To himself*) It can't fail! Now to show him who's boss around here . . . (*To second servant*) Well, you numbskull, don't you see we need chairs?

(*Second servant brings two chairs.*)

Lard (*continuing*): And now disappear, and don't listen at the door.

(*Second servant leaves through center.*)

Vincelli (*to himself*): Incredible . . . such vulgarity!

(*Both men sit down.*)

Lard: I tell you, my dear Bintchelli, servants give me a headache! And I have fifteen. How many do you have?

Vincelli: Never mind. Let us talk of the affair that has forced me . . .

Lard: Oh, you mean your son's marriage . . .

Vincelli: Marriage? I trust you see how impossible such a union would be.

LARD: Impossible? Why impossible? Of course, I don't know what he sees in her, but you know how it is — if a young billy wants to tangle, there's nothing the old goat can do about it.

VINCELLI (*to himself*): And with this person my son wants to enter into family relations . . . (*To Lard*) My dear man, don't you forget the difference in rank . . .

LARD (*getting angry*): Balderdash! You still have a long way to go to the Emperor of Morocco. And she's the one who got the treasury.

VINCELLI (*to himself*): Shades of my ancestors . . . treasury . . . it's abominable!

LARD: Besides, all these shenanigans are none of my business . . .

VINCELLI (*to himself*): Shenanigans. I feel faint.

LARD: It's all up to Lucia Thistle . . .

VINCELLI: Lucia Thistle — what a name!

LARD: Don't worry about the name. When she marries your son she'll be a Bintchelli.

VINCELLI: No, it can't be. It has to be prevented at all costs. (*To Lard, in a more conciliatory tone*) Listen, my friend —

LARD: Well, that's better! (*Slapping Vincelli's knee*) That's the kind of chin music I like to hear!

VINCELLI (*shuddering*): Heavens! (*Taking hold of himself, to Lard*) Tell me frankly, do you expect pecuniary gain from this matter?

LARD: You — now I almost called you a ninnyhammer. Do you think I need money? Look, that's like carrying schnitzels to Vienna. But to tell you the truth, I'm not so keen on your son marrying Lucia. If you really want to upset their applecart I'll lend you a hand. Talk to your son; better still, talk to Lucia first. I'll send her in.

VINCELLI: Very good. Do that, my good man. (*Stands up.*)

LARD (*also rising*): See, I'm not such a bad egg. We'll get along. Just wait here, Brother Chinelli. I'll send Lucia in here in two shakes of a lamb's tail!

(Exits through side left.)

Scene 12

VINCELLI (*alone*):   This will take ten years off my life. The vulgarity of this jackanapes gives me convulsions — it makes me choke, I'll have to relieve my blood pressure with leeches, purge myself in a steam bath, take the mineral waters, purify my soul by prolonged etiquette. They say the girl is enchanting. Her beauty is the basis of the renegade's false hopes. But I'm fortified, ready to block even the most heavenly creature from the house of Vincelli . . . listen . . . here . . . I believe I hear the steps of his idol!

Scene 13

LUCIA (*entering from the side left, sees Vincelli, to herself*): So that's my young man's old man? My brother-in-law says he's a marquis . . . how does one address a marquis? (*Makes a curtsy to Vincelli.*) I kiss your hand, Your Honor.

VINCELLI (*nodding lightly, to himself*):   I wonder who that is?

LUCIA: My brother-in-law has told me that you found out about your son's marriage plan, and that you are lukewarm about it . . .

VINCELLI (*to himself*):   The story is all over the place. (*To Lucia*) Do you know my son?

LUCIA (*coquettish*):   I'll say! (*To herself*) That's a batty question!

VINCELLI (*to himself*): He seems to have confided in all members of this common family. (*To Lucia*) You met my son here at the mansion?

LUCIA: No, your Marquisship, last summer at the penny-a-dance ball.

VINCELLI (*to himself*): Horrors!

LUCIA: Your son is quite a dancer — we got first prize in the hog-wrestle . . .

VINCELLI: Spirits of my forefathers! (*Covers his face with his hands.*)

LUCIA: Well, why not? A little bouse doesn't do any harm. It's not that he is jug-bitten.

VINCELLI: Jug-bitten! (*Wrings his hands.*) Too much! Too much!

LUCIA: Oh, I wouldn't worry about that. You'd be surprised how much he can take!

VINCELLI (*with effort*): Pardon me, my time is limited. I am expecting a young woman by the name of Lucia Thistle —

LUCIA: That's my name.

VINCELLI: Then it must be your daughter I'm expecting.

LUCIA: What — daughter?

VINCELLI: A young girl, Lucia Thistle.

LUCIA: I'm the only Thistle in Lower Austria.

VINCELLI: There must be some mistake. The young girl I wish to see is the one my son is courting, under an assumed name. She has been described to me as a gentle, lovely creature of unusual beauty.

LUCIA: Why, yes — that's me.

VINCELLI (*automatically*): Impossible!

LUCIA (*with rising anger*): Why impossible, I'd like to know? And what do you mean, daughter? How dare you wish a daughter on me, you pinhead!

VINCELLI (*to himself*): Gentle and lovely — heavens! (*To*

Lucia) I didn't mean to offend you. Please tell me: has my son seriously promised to marry you?

LUCIA: A marriage proposal is no laughing matter. His voice definitely had an engagement ring in it.

VINCELLI (*walking desperately up and down*): My son has lost his mind!

LUCIA: Oh, stop looking down your nose — it gives you the wrong slant. If you don't want to give your permission . . .

VINCELLI: Oh, Lord! Never! I've already told Lard . . .

LUCIA: Oh? Well, I'll tell you something, too: we'll get married without your permission. Your son's of age and I — I've lost my birth certificate, so no one can prove that I'm too young. Your son doesn't care whether you disown him or not, he's told me so. We'll live off my money. So there! My daughter — I've never been so insulted in my life! (*With a short curtsy*) Good day!

(*Exits left.*)

Scene 14

VINCELLI (*alone*): Is this a nightmare? To love this person — unimaginable! And yet — his own admission — and the person herself confirmed it. What a tragedy — a Vincelli has lost his mind! This has never happened in our family. (*Reflecting, walking up and down*) Alfred is stubborn — there's only one way to avoid disaster. The person doesn't seem to care about rank or money, she wants a young man. Lard must find a suitable commoner whom I will give twenty- or thirty-thousand thalers, on condition that he marry the person on the spot. Lard will help — he wants to ingratiate himself with me. But it's difficult for me to talk to the man — I shall write to him, a dignified, cordial letter asking him to do me this favor — yes, that's the best way. I shall return to the inn. Oh dear, why must I go to that inn? I'd rather sit for an hour at the tomb of my forebears, surrounded by lofty decay, to purge myself from the vulgar air I was forced to breathe here.

> (*Exits through the center, fanning himself with his handkerchief.*)

Scene 15

> (*Room in the left wing of the mansion, same as in Act Two, Scene 6.*)

FERDINAND (*to Moon*):   It's not true, it can't be true! Confess, you've told me a cock-and-bull story!

MOON: Not I, it's Miss Fritzi who's doing the cock-and-bulling. When she swore to you about love and sighed about eternal devotion — *that* was cock and bull.

FERDINAND (*desperate*):   My Fritzi — it's beyond imagination!

MOON: I wouldn't have imagined it myself. But as soon as I told her I was a baron, the seeds of treachery began sprouting in her mind. Her face reddened, her hopes rose to sky blue, and the purple of passion blended with the green of envy. It was such a display of color, no wonder the future now looks pale to you.

FERDINAND: No, it can't be. I'm not vain, but I'm not bad looking — I can't believe she'd go for that censored face of yours, for that stork figure!

MOON: That's the magic of the baronage.

FERDINAND: I must have proof, or . . .

MOON (*has looked back to the right*):   Quiet, here she comes now!

FERDINAND: Fritzi?

MOON: It's terrible, how this woman chases me!

FERDINAND: I burst — I choke — how can she . . .

MOON: Here is your chance to know the truth. Quick, into this room, put your ear to the keyhole, and you'll hear the story from her own lips.

FERDINAND: All right, I'll do it.

MOON (*at the door left*): I'd better lock you in so that you won't pop out until she's gone.

FERDINAND: I promise . . . By my honor!

MOON: I'd rather trust the lock! (*He pushes Ferdinand through door at left and locks it.*)

Scene 16

MOON (*alone*): Now comes the double thumbscrew as planned. (*Goes to meet Fritzi at the arch.*)

FRITZI: Baron, my maid told me . . .

MOON (*takes her quickly to the foreground right, in low voice*): Quiet, your earthly maker is listening! (*Points at the door left. The following is spoken quickly and softly.*)

FRITZI: Papa?

MOON: He's hopping mad, he's boiling. He is about to have your fiancé chucked out of here by the scruff of his neck, and even said something about not sparing the rod on your charming blind cheeks.

FRITZI (*frightened*): Oh no, he wouldn't do that to his obedient daughter!

MOON: I succeeded in calming him . . .

FRITZI: Oh, you're an angel!

MOON: . . . even persuaded him to consent to your marriage with Buchner.

FRITZI: Oh, you're a devil!

MOON: But only on condition that you prove your daughterly obedience . . .

FRITZI: Oh, gladly!

MOON: . . . by declaring first that you'll give up your lover and agree to marry me.

FRITZI: What?

MOON: Only pretending, of course.

FRITZI: What do you mean?

MOON: Your father has old-fashioned ideas about daughterly obedience. He is not so much against Ferdinand as against your disobeying Papa. He doesn't want you to marry Ferdinand, so if you convince Papa that you won't, the obstacle is removed and you can marry Ferdinand. But if you insist on marrying Ferdinand you can't. Is that clear?

FRITZI   You mean . . . ?

MOON: If you say no, it's yes, and if you say yes, it's no. So let's humor Papa. Come close to the door. I'll have to ask you some embarrassing questions but remember — if you pass these finals you'll graduate in a cap and gown with a bridal veil attached. (*He leads her to the door left and talks very loudly.*) Then you are prepared, Miss Fritzi, to respect the wishes of your father?

FRITZI (*loudly*):   With daughterly obedience, yes.

MOON (*softly*):   Very good but a little louder, please. (*Loudly*) You know that he has offered me your dainty little hand?

FRITZI (*disgusted*):   Ugh!

MOON (*softly*):   Don't forget yourself! (*Aloud*) But my principles won't permit me to accept that hand unless, as on a charm bracelet, a heart is attached.

FRITZI: I understand.

MOON: May I hope then that I can win your heart? You

look at me? You blush? You press my hand to your heaving bosom? An amorous sigh, half suppressed yet with significant eloquence, escapes your tremulous breast?

FRITZI (*softly*): Aren't you putting it on too thickly?

MOON (*softly*): Just for Papa's benefit. (*Aloud*) Oh, I understand . . . you speak the language of the soul, not with your lips, but with your eyes, and you promise me bliss beyond words! (*The noise of a chair being tossed to the floor is heard from the room to the left.*)

FRITZI (*softly*): What's Papa doing?

MOON (*softly*): Everything's fine. That's the prearranged signal of his satisfaction. (*Aloud*) But I still have Ferdinand Buchner on my conscience . . . he's such a fine young man, poor but honest . . . and in love with you. Therefore, pray, tell me . . . How do you feel about him?

FRITZI: If Papa says so, I'll let Ferdinand go.

MOON (*softly*): Good. (*Aloud*) Then you don't love him?

FRITZI (*forgetting herself*): Oh, yes! (*Moon gestures to her.*) No, I meant to say. A child should never love anyone his father doesn't approve of. (*A similar but stronger noise from the room to the left*)

MOON (*softly*): Your father is getting happier by the minute. (*Aloud*) Then I may tell your father that you'll give up Herr Buchner without a protest?

FRITZI (*sighing, but then aloud*): Without a protest!

MOON: And sign a marriage contract with me right away?

FRITZI: As Papa wishes.

MOON: And follow me willingly into the bridal chamber?

FRITZI (*softly*): No, I won't answer that!

MOON (*aloud*): You remain silent? Your eyelashes flutter? And a bashful rosy dawn announces the morning tide of love?

FRITZI (*softly*): But, Baron . . .

MOON (*with rising display of emotion*): A fervid tear

springs from your bewildered eye? Oh, let me kiss it from
your cheeks, this precious pearl, this superheavenly witness
of an emotional underground erruption! (*Takes her hand
and kisses it several times very loudly.*)

FRITZI (*softly and very uneasily*): Baron, what are you . . .
(*A violent crash from the room at the left.*)

MOON (*softly*): You hear? Your father is beside himself
with delight. (*To himself*) Now I have to get her out of
here before he smashes all the furniture. (*Aloud*) That will
do, sweet bride, your willingnesss ought to convince the
most stubborn doubter. You have shown yourself an obedient daughter — (*Softly while leading her back to the
arch*) — and have only played a little comedy which will
go far to help your leading man. But strictest silence — or
it's curtains!

FRITZI: Oh yes, Baron, yes! (*Rushes off through the center.*)

MOON (*to himself*): The show's made me hot but I bet my
friend in there is steamed up even more. (*Unlocking the
door left*) She's gone, Herr Buchner, you may come out.

Scene 17

(*Ferdinand bursts into the room, his tie undone,
his hair wild, his vest open, a pistol in his hand.*)

FERDINAND: Heaven and earth, what have I heard! Do I
still have a head that can think? Can my feet still kick, my
teeth still gnash?

MOON: That's how they are, those women!

FERDINAND: The most monstrous deed has been done, and
the earth doesn't tumble, and the skies look down in
apathy! What are you hanging up there for, you stupid

clouds, if you can't storm and thunder at the right time?

MOON: Herr Buchner . . .

FERDINAND: But thank God, there's thunder in here! (*Raising the pistol*) It's loaded!

MOON (*noticing the pistol*): No! Don't shoot!

FERDINAND (*beside himself*): Shoot I will, but whom?

MOON (*getting more frightened*): Whom do you suggest?

FFRDINAND: The faithless woman, myself, or you!

MOON: Me? Why me?

FERDINAND: Three people and only one shot! Three targets and only one bullet!

MOON (*trying to take the pistol away from him*): Allow me . . .

FERDINAND: I can't go in! I'll be selfish and shoot myself.

MOON (*trying to prevent it*): Don't do anything foolish!

FERDINAND: Let me go!

(*They wrestle; the pistol is accidentally fired in the air.*)

MOON: Ooooh! (*Collapses in fright.*)

FERDINAND: What have I done? Moon — Moon — show a sign . . . I've killed him! (*Drops the pistol.*)

Scene 18

LARD (*coming through the arch left*): What was that? A shot . . . ah, the young marquis! Dead! Murdered . . . here . . . in my home! Holla there! Help! Servants, family, hired hands!

LUCIA (*entering with Ulrike*): That was a shot! Ah, my fiancé! (*Falls into a faint in Ulrike's arms.*)

LARD: The noble offspring — shot down!

MOON: Not every bullet finds its mark . . . (*Raising himself*)
But it was close!

LUCIA: His voice? He's alive!

MOON: Just a little moonstruck, my dear Lucia!

LARD: What's that? Were you just scared?

MOON (*a bit embarrassed*):   I always feel funny if someone
shoots at the Moon.

FRITZI (*coming through the arch*):   What happened?

FERDINAND (*as if waking from a stupor*):   You . . . don't
come near me . . .

FRITZI: Ferdinand! Let me tell you . . .

FERDINAND (*furiously*):   Hypocrite! Monster! Snake! It's all
over, everything is over! (*Runs through the arch left.*)

FRITZI: He's leaving me . . . (*Faints into Ulrike's arms.*)

ULRIKE: Fritzi! There must be some misunderstanding . . .

LARD: Child! Fritzi! Wake up! What is all this?

MOON (*taking him aside*):   I have carried out my scheme of
separation . . .

LARD (*extremely surprised*):   So fast . . . ? Marquis . . .
(*Shaking his hand*) my congratulations! I don't know how
you did it!

MOON (*with affected modesty*):   The hand is quicker than
the eye!

(*Music.*)

CURTAIN

ACT THREE

(Room in the Silver Stallion Inn)

Scene 1

(Moon enters hurriedly through the center, with wife of the Innkeeper.)

MOON: The Innkeeper isn't home? Good!

WIFE OF INNKEEPER: What is it all about?

MOON: Oh, little things, about a little bullet and a little hole in my little skull.

WIFE *(frightened)*: You don't mean —

MOON *(indicating shooting)*: Yes, I do. It was my master's idea. But now I trust he has calmed down enough to be satisfied with merely breaking a few of my bones. But even this modification has no appeal for me so I've decided to do a little cubbyholing. But where? Then I had a flash — *(In solemn tone)* — the place where you owe 286 thalers and 36 groschen, that's the place where you are safe — no one will look for you there! *(In normal voice)* You see how a resourceful man makes use even of his debts.

WIFE: But what will my husband say?

MOON: That stands to reason, what an innkeeper will say to a guest of my paying power. But what a wife will say to an innkeeper so he'll keep such a guest, only her heart can tell.

235

WIFE (*pouting*):   Oh, go on, you wicked man. You don't deserve . . .

MOON: Repentance will soften up even the gods . . . (*Chivalrous*) . . . should a goddess prove unforgiving?

WIFE: Oh, what a line you have!

MOON: Innkeeperess, be noble!

WIFE: There's only one way: You'd have to give my husband a partial payment.

MOON: I can see what you're aiming at. Give your generosity free rein!

WIFE: I'll lend you a hundred thalers . . .

MOON: Oh divine creditress . . . how delightful to fall head over heels in debt with you!

WIFE: Now stop that and go to your room (*Wagging a finger coquettishly*) and don't show your face . . . we have a very high-born guest.

MOON: What's that got to do with me?

WIFE: Stay out of trouble and in your room, so I can find you when I have the hundred thalers.

MOON: You'll find me, angel of mercy! Money may not make a person happy but it keeps his creditors in a good mood!

(*Moon exits back left, Innkeeper's wife back right.*)

Scene 2

(*Vincelli and Alfred enter from right front, arguing heatedly.*)

VINCELLI: I want to hear no more!

ALFRED: This is unbelievable — have you really seen her?

VINCELLI: Seen and heard, I'm chagrined to say.

ALFRED: Father, I have . . .

VINCELLI: You have no eyes, no ears, no taste, no breeding! Begone!

ALFRED: You drive me to desperation! Do you want to see me hang from the next oak tree?

VINCELLI: No, but neither do I want to see this woman hang on our family tree. (*Threateningly*) Remember the penny-a-dance day!

ALFRED (*amazed*):   What . . . ?

VINCELLI: What do you care? Remember the hog-wrestle!

ALFRED: But, Father . . .

VINCELLI: You wrestled our family honor into the dirt!

ALFRED: There must be some mistake! You cannot possibly have seen her, Father!

VINCELLI: She confessed that you promised to marry her. But hold no hopes!

ALFRED: Father, my life depends on this marriage! I'm heartbroken to resist you . . . but I can't help myself!

(*Exits through center.*)

Scene 3

VINCELLI: He's mad . . . what can I do? (*Takes an open letter from his pocket.*)   Lard writes me that he knows a poor devil who will marry the person for the sum I offered. I have to act quickly; much as it disgusts me I have to go and see that boor once more! (*Starts to leave, but runs into the Innkeeper.*)

INNKEEPER (*entering with letter in hand*):   Beg your pardon, Your Excellency, I didn't know . . .

VINCELLI: Is this letter for me?

INNKEEPER: No, Your Excellency. It's a very ordinary letter from Miss Lucia Thistle to . . .

VINCELLI: To the young man who is courting her?

INNKEEPER: With your permissison, Your Excellency.

VINCELLI: I suppose he doesn't use his real name?

INNKEEPER: No, he calls himself Baron Moonbeam . . . But his real name is . . .

VINCELLI: Don't say it. I want to avoid at any price that the name be mentioned.

INNKEEPER: I didn't realize that Your Excellency was interested in . . .

VINCELLI: Give me that letter!

INNKEEPER: My humblest apologies, but I have no right to do that, and if I may be so bold as to point out ever so meekly, not even Your Excellency . . .

VINCELLI: Unfortunately, I'm more than entitled to see the letter — I'm his father.

INNKEEPER (*extremely amazed*):   What? Your Excellency — his father?

VINCELLI: Do I have to repeat what I'd like to conceal? The young man is my son.

INNKEEPER: Well, if that's the case, I can only say, "Your Excellency!" (*Gives him the letter with a deep bow. To himself*) Moon told me that his illegitimate father may be very blue-nosed; and I believed that he was just a gyp of an old block.

VINCELLI: You may go.

INNKEEPER: As you please . . . only I'd like to drop the most subtle hint, if I may do so without arousing Your Excellency's displeasure, that the young gentleman owes me 286 thalers and 36 groschen.

VINCELLI: Put it on my bill.

INNKEEPER: Hooray! (*Pulling himself together*) . . . I would have said if it were not (*Bowing deeply*) against etiquette. (*To himself*) Tooty-tooty, that's the kind of father to have! Wait till I tell my little woman, she's such a romantic soul.

(*Exits through center.*)

Scene 4

VINCELLI: What horrors shall I read here? (*Opens letter and drops envelope on the floor.*) Pink paper . . . cheap perfume . . . signs of vulgarity everywhere. (*Reads*) "My dear and only bobolink! You left like (*Slowly deciphering*) bricksy . . . wicksy . . . so I could not tell you that I and your old man had quite a tussle . . . he's an old sumph . . ." Dreadful! (*Continues reading*) "He insulted me and I told him we would get married, and he could sit on his money until it hatches . . ." Abominable! (*Reading*) "Let's whip off tonight before your puffed-up father can poke his dusty nose into our affair. The Innkeeper has good horses. Elopingly yours, Lucia." (*In great excitement*) Shame! Disgrace! Elopement! (*He rings the bell.*) That plan must be nipped in the bud!

Scene 5

INNKEEPER: Your Excellency!

VINCELLI: Does my son have a wagon and horses?

INNKEEPER: No trace of a wagon, no thought of a horse!

VINCELLI: Good. But you have horses?

INNKEEPER: Four of them, genuine Slovak thoroughbreds, first-class chestnut tough hides, trained for plow, saddle, stagecoach or brick wagon — they handle everything.

VINCELLI: I need no horses.

INNKEEPER: Yes, I know, Your Excellency has his own.

VINCELLI: My son will order horses, but *I* order you not to let him have any. I have reasons to keep him here.

INNKEEPER: My entire stable will be lame. None of the horses will be able to take a step.

VINCELLI: Good. (*To himself*) There, my fine young heir, now I have . . . in the language of your sweetheart . . . poked my dusty nose into your affairs. (*Leaving*) Now I must overcome my distaste and see Lard. (*Innkeeper opens center door with a deep bow. Outside, a servant who accompanies Vincelli.*)

Scene 6

INNKEEPER: Now this is a side of the moon no one has seen yet!

MOON (*from side door left, to himself*):   I forgot to tell her . . . uh-uh, trouble! (*Aloud*) I know what you're going to say, and it will all spell 286 thalers and 36 groschen!

INNKEEPER: Not at all. Let's not talk about it.

MOON: That suits me, I'd be willing to forgive and forget but . . .

INNKEEPER: If I alluded this morning to some sort of claim . . .

MOON: I vaguely recall you did call me a swindler and came after me with coppers . . . but I don't remember the details.

INNKEEPER: Please, forget it.

MOON: Don't worry, I've never developed much of a memory concerning my debts. But whom do I thank for this change of attitude?

INNKEEPER: Your father, of course.

MOON (*puzzled*):   My father?

INNKEEPER: The Marquis de Vincelli.

MOON: Listen, if this is a joke, it is on you. It's you who'll be out of the 286 thalers.

INNKEEPER: I wish you owed me twice that much.

MOON (*holding out his hand*): I'm willing to cooperate.

INNKEEPER: No, that wouldn't be fair to His Excellency. He's underwritten enough for you.

MOON (*delighted*): To underwrite a man who's been written off as a credit risk everywhere except on the black-lists of innkeepers — only a father can do this unselfish deed — I'm beginning to believe it! Oh, Mother, your sin turns out to be a blessing! (*Notices the envelope on the floor.*) What's this? (*Picks up the envelope and reads*) "To the Honorable Baron Moonbeam —" To me? Opened? And only the envelope? That's Lucia's scrawl. Where is the letter?

INNKEEPER: Your father has it.

MOON: You know what it said?

INNKEEPER: It must have waxed very elopishly, for His Excellency ordered strictest embargo on my horses.

MOON: How this man concerns himself with my affairs — but, of course, as my father . . .

INNKEEPER: He was so angry about your love affair, he was about to jump out of his skin.

MOON: Not a very practical way out of a problem.

INNKEEPER: Your father is right. This Thistle woman is not for you.

MOON: I'm going up to the mansion . . .

INNKEEPER: Don't you want to change your collar . . . ?

MOON: Right. I no longer need the disguise. Do you have the piece I ripped off?

INNKEEPER: My wife's kept it.

MOON: Good, ask her to sew it back on again. (*As he turns to leave, Alfred enters through the middle. Moon greets him very casually and condescendingly.*) Good day, Secretary, good day!

(*Exits right.*)

Scene 7

ALFRED (*to himself*): Is this fellow drunk? (*To Innkeeper*) You have horses?

INNKEEPER: Do you need them to drive out or to stay in? To stay in I've already rented them to the Marquis.

ALFRED: What do you mean?

INNKEEPER: He intercepted a letter from a certain female to his son . . .

ALFRED (*puzzled, to himself*): A letter from Ulrike to me?

INNKEEPER: . . . and told me not to let his son have them.

ALFRED (*hesitantly*): But . . . you will rent them to *me*?

INNKEEPER: To you? Of course. That makes sense.

ALFRED (*under his breath*): Horse sense! (*Aloud*) As soon as it gets dark, have the carriage ready behind the Lard mansion. Be on time and discreet! (*Gives him money.*)

INNKEEPER: On time, discreet, and in raptures.

ALFRED (*to himself*): What can Ulrike have written to me? I have to talk to her! (*Exits through center.*)

INNKEEPER: He also has something brewing up at the mansion. Doesn't Lard notice . . . or doesn't he want to? That's the puzzler posed a thousand times a day and that's so hard to figure out: doesn't he want to notice, or is he really so stupid?

> (*Exits through center, shaking his head.*)

Scene 8

MOON (*coming from the right*): The traces of the servant are covered. Now I've got to find out for sure whether I have a father or a *fata morgana*. I have to be careful and discard my Lucia queen of hearts only if I can count on my papa ace up my sleeve. I'm still treading on sand, and it would be poppycock for a wanderer in the desert to pour away even brackish water before he's found a clear well. But, of course, the world is full of poppycock notions.

SONG

The daughter is pretty, her mother is vain.
The girl has a lover, and he has a brain.
And just as a thief bribes a watchdog with wienies,
The boy tells the mother that her face like nineteen is.
The mother is tickled, and he is allowed
To do as he pleases — she walks on a cloud.
"I am quite a dish to arouse such emotion!"
    That's a poppycock notion!

"Pray, who was that man with your wife whom I saw?"
"Oh, he is all right, that's her brother-in-law."
"They stood in a doorway, she tickled his jaw."
"What's wrong with her tickling her brother-in-law?"
"They went to the brook for a swim in the raw!"
"Why shouldn't they swim — he's her brother-in-law!
If he were not an in-law, I would stop such devotion!"
    That's a poppycock notion!

A woman is fat so she's taking a pill.
A man wants sweet breath so he eats chlorophyll.
A lotion each night makes you young when you're not.
If your bust needs a boom have a silicone shot.
A happiness pill makes you happy and gay,
And a tablet a day keeps the babies away.
All problems are solved by a pill or a lotion:
    That's a poppycock notion!

ENCORE

I dreamed of a world which forgot how to add.
Where no one had money, but all spent like mad.
You bought, threw away, bought a different style,
They ran after you, gave you loans with a smile.
And if you paid cash even just for a schnapps
You'd think the whole country was about to collapse.
You could buy a new house without having a groschen —
    That's a poppycock notion!

(Exits.)

Scene 9

*(Garden behind the mansion. In the foreground,
right, the back entrance to a garden house; in the
foreground left, part of a wall with a gate.)*

PHILIPPINA *(talking to Ferdinand)*:   I don't believe it. It's
not like Miss Fritzi.

FERDINAND: But it's true. If her ugly character had shown
in her face, I'd never have fallen in love with her. But
now I'll keep away from her, I'll avoid her like . . .

PHILIPPINA: Is that why you run around under her window
like a drunk rooster?

FERDINAND: If she comes down I'll go to the far end of the
garden.

PHILIPPINA: She'll follow you.

FERDINAND: Then I'll run into the street.

PHILIPPINA: She'll run after you.

FERDINAND: Then I'll run to Vienna.

PHILIPPINA: And into the arms of another woman? Well,
that would be the end of the run-around. I wouldn't care
to predict what Miss Fritzi would do then.

FERDINAND: I know what she would do. She'd marry the Baron.

PHILIPPINA (*puzzled*): What gives you that idea?

FERDINAND: I was hidden in a room . . .

PHILIPPINA: *You* were in that room?

FERDINAND: And I heard with my own ears . . .

PHILIPPINA (*looking at him doubtfully*): Nothing is as deceptive as a man's ears.

FERDINAND: Why are you looking at me as if you thought my ears were too short?

PHILIPPINA: I won't answer leading questions. You want me to give Miss Fritzi a message?

FERDINAND: Tell her that she's lost to me forever, and that she'll never see me again. Tell her that!

PHILIPPINA: All right, I'll tell her that. And in the meantime you stay right here in the dark garden so you can be sure she won't see you. (*Watching him half in pity, half in mockery*) Oh, you men, you are young only once, but you can stay babies forever!

(*Exits through the center.*)

Scene 10

FERDINAND (*alone*): Did she mean me?

LARD (*from the garden house*): Buchner, I want to talk to you.

FERDINAND: I have to apologize, Herr von Lard.

LARD: What for?

FERDINAND: For disturbing the peace of your. home with that shot.

LARD: Oh well, guns will go off, it can happen to anybody.

FERDINAND: Your kindness surprises me.

LARD: I've got an even bigger surprise for you. How would
you like to get 20,000 thalers?

FERDINAND: 20,000 thalers? That's a ticklish question.

LARD: I can make it even more ticklish: how would you
like 30,000?

FERDINAND: Whom do I have to kill this time?

LARD: Only two birds with one stone.

FERDINAND: What do I have to do?

LARD: Just say the word. Two little words: I — do.

FERDINAND: You torment me, and that doesn't tickle, that
rubs me the wrong way.

LARD: No, seriously. You want to get married anyway. How
would you like to get 30,000 thalers for it — dowry, damages, whatever you prefer to call it.

FERDINAND: Heavens! How terrible . . . what has she done?

LARD: What has who done?

FERDINAND (*wringing his hands*): Has she sunk so low that
you want to pay 30,000 thalers to someone just so he will
marry this sweet, dear creature?

LARD: Never mind the sweet and dear — think of the money
which, by the way, won't be paid by me but by old Tchinelli.

FERDINAND: Why does Vincelli want me to marry your
daughter?

LARD: Who's talking of my daughter, you numbskull!

FERDINAND (*startled*): Whom do you want me to marry,
then?

LARD: The one his son is so crazy about. Tchinelli doesn't
like it, so he's ready to pay cash to find someone who will
take her off the market.

FERDINAND (*amazed, to himself*): Ulrike? The girl's a
beauty, but . . .

LARD: Are you considering?

FERDINAND: I'm starting to.

LARD: All right, be quick about it.

FERDINAND (*to himself*): No, she's Alfred's bride, only a rat would . . . and yet . . .

LARD (*impatiently*): Are you still considering?

FERDINAND: Just a moment. (*To himself*) It would be a sweet revenge on Fritzi . . . a true revenge on a false heart . . . I'd only pretend, of course.

LARD (*angrily*): I can help you make up your mind . . .

FERDINAND: Give me another second . . . (*Steps aside and gesticulates as he continues thinking.*)

LARD (*after a moment*): Come on, I don't have all day . . .

FERDINAND (*to himself*): A glorious way to get even! (*To Lard*) Tell the Marquis . . .

LARD (*harshly*): Yes or no?

FERDINAND: Yes!

LARD: It's a deal.

FERDINAND: I'm prepared . . .

LARD: You are prepared to marry — that's all my good friend, the Marquis, wants to know. Now don't go away, so we can find you when we need you for the wedding!

(*Exits into the garden house.*)

Scene 11

FERDINAND (*alone*): I feel giddy — but why should I? I said yes to Lard . . . that doesn't count — as long as I haven't said it to Ulrike in front of the priest . . .

ULRIKE (*entering from right*): Herr Buchner, I've been looking for you . . .

FERDINAND (*frightened, to himself*): Oh, Lord, she already knows.

ULRIKE: . . . to ask you to do me an act of friendship.

FERDINAND (*to himself*): She calls marriage an act of friendship?

ULRIKE: Alfred has deceived me about his rank, and now he feels guilty and keeps away from me. Please tell him not to worry. Tell him that I give up any claim on him.

FERDINAND (*getting scared*): You do? You won't marry Alfred? That means you're ready to marry someone else . . .

ULRIKE (*too preoccupied with her thoughts to pay attention to his words*): It's not that I feel unworthy to be his wife. No man stands so high that he's disgraced by a girl's unselfish love. But I don't want to stand between him and his father.

FERDINAND (*moved*): You are sweet. You make it really hard on me just to pretend . . .

ULRIKE (*puzzled*): What do you mean?

FERDINAND (*a bit embarrassed*): You know, of course, the plan which the old Marquis and Lard have concocted?

ULRIKE: Not a word.

FERDINAND: Two words, as he put it, which we are supposed to exchange . . .

ULRIKE: You don't mean that we are to . . .

FERDINAND: Yes, we are, and today.

ULRIKE: It must be a joke.

FERDINAND: The old Vincelli doesn't joke. He's paying a heap of money if I'll do it.

ULRIKE: Oh, I see through their scheme. It's an outrage how these noble gentlemen think they can manipulate human hearts with money!

FERDINAND: They mostly succeed.

ULRIKE: But not always!

FERDINAND: I, for my part, agreed . . .

ULRIKE (*surprised, stepping back*): Herr Buchner . . .

FERDINAND: . . . to spite Fritzi. I'm taking a desperate chance. Besides, it *is* difficult to refuse someone like you.

ULRIKE: You're very gracious. And this gives me the courage to ask you one more favor.

FERDINAND: Granted!

ULRIKE: When you see the Marquis, please give him this picture. (*Gives him a locket.*)

FERDINAND (*taking it*): Certainly.

ULRIKE: In return for your kindness, may I offer my good services for an understanding between you and Fritzi?

FERDINAND (*irritable*): No services needed.

ULRIKE (*laughing*): Well, you were ready to marry me to get her back. Maybe it can be done less painfully. I'll send her here.

FERDINAND: No, no, don't do that. I'll leave — I'll hide in the bushes where no one can find me, and never come out. (*Rushes off to the left.*)

ULRIKE (*alone*): I know how he feels. I too would like to crawl in a hole and never show my face again.

(*Exits at right.*)

Scene 12

(*The stage is empty. From behind the garden wall one hears the same two chords Moon plucked on his guitar in Act Two.*)

LARD (*coming out of the garden house*): Heavens! The reckless virtuoso! What if his father recognizes him by his tune? (*Crosses the stage, unlocks the gate in the wall and opens it.*)

MOON (*a guitar in his hand, enters quickly*): Coo-ee! Donna Lucia!

LARD: Quiet, for heaven's sakes!

MOON: Oh, it's you.

LARD: Do you know who is here?

MOON: I've heard parental rumors.

LUCIA (*right, offstage*): Where are you, lovebird?

MOON: Here, Lucia! (*Quickly plays his two chords.*)

LARD: Hush. Cut the concert! (*Holds his hand to the strings of the guitar.*) The Marquis is sitting in front of the garden house.

MOON: I want to talk to him. (*Tries to enter garden house.*)

LARD: Not yet! First get rid of her, and fast! (*Points in the direction of Lucia.*) I'm straightening things out for you . . . me and my pal, His Excellency. You wait here.

(*Exits into the garden house.*)

Scene 13

MOON (*alone*): I have to know if I am a blue blood or a blue Moon . . .

LUCIA (*from the right*): Here I am, I heard your guitar. See how I am trained to answer when you call me?

MOON: Yes, my dear mynah bird.

LUCIA: It's so romantic — the way you play the guitar! Is it a concert piece or an improvisation?

MOON: It's a variation. First this (*Plays one chord.*) — then this. (*Plays the second chord.*) The beauty lies in the alteration.

LUCIA: You are a rare man!

MOON (*very fondly*): Oh, you celestial night bird, you heavenly owl! (*To himself*) I won't quit being the lover until I'm sure that I'm the son.

LUCIA: So you got my letter?

MOON: No, my little warbler.

Lucia: How's that possible?

Moon: It's been snatched, my pied wagtail.

Lucia: I can imagine by whom.

Moon: Who, my pink-breasted chat? Tell me.

Lucia: By your spiteful father, the stuck-up Marquis.

Moon: Then you know that Marquis Vincelli is my father?

Lucia: He told me so himself.

Moon (*growing colder*): So you talked to him?

Lucia: Yes, and a lot of good it did me. That silver spoon he was born with hasn't stirred him up. But I did, believe you me. I even upset the family tree he keeps balanced on his nose. I told him we'd elope.

Moon: Elope? I don't know . . .

Lucia: You don't know? (*Silence. They both look at each other.*) What's the matter? Why don't you say something?

Moon: I'm a man of few words, so I don't have to take many of them back. Right now, my heart wavers between love and duty. (*Feigns an inner struggle.*)

Lucia: You more likely mean love and booty . . . But I tell you, if you know what's good for you . . .

Moon: I know . . . (*Ostentatiously*) . . . what a good son must do!

Lucia: Now, listen . . .

Moon: Yes, I must listen to my head, not my heart.

Lucia: And when money speaks you don't miss a word, do you? Well, if you think I'll give you up now, you're not only a Moon, you're a lunatic!

Moon: If a father says "No marriage," a good son will never Mrs. anybody.

Lucia: So that's the time of day, is it?

Moon: Yes it's ten minutes past a quarter to good-bye.

Lucia: Your affection dies quickly, doesn't it? Well, mine doesn't. I have a written promise of marriage. My affections will sue, they will go through all the courts of appeal, and will insist on a verdict . . . and if there's any justice in the land, that will be in my favor! (*Exits at right in great excitement.*)

MOON: Heavens! You don't know how explosive women are until you drop one! But now I have a father to take care of all my problems. A dozen women could sue me now, it wouldn't worry me — he's rich enough to buy them maternity dresses and settle paternity suits. I leave it all to him — a son need not think that just because he's of age, he has to be too independent!

Scene 14

LARD (*coming from the garden house*): I've got to talk to you, son of the upper four hundred . . . it's for your best. Do you realize what it means to lose a father?

MOON: No, I'm barely beginning to realize what it means to find one. (*To Lard*) Hasn't he mentioned my late mother, Nina?

LARD: No.

MOON: But his actions speak louder than words. No doubt he was the mysterious man in the Moon.

LARD: *You* are the mystery. I cannot see what you find so hot about Lucia.

MOON: Frankly, the only thing hot about her is her temper.

LARD: You're cured, offspring of the upper crust! You make sense again! Thank goodness that your love melts away so easily!

MOON: It waxes and wanes — a characteristic that runs in the family.

LARD: I can't believe it — you wanted to die with that person!

MOON: Dying is easy, that's over in a second. But I wanted to live with her for years — that's real proof of devotion!

LARD: How did you get rid of her?

MOON: Womenfolk are full of contrariness — when she saw I let her down, she upped and left.

LARD: She wasn't right for you anyway, the silly goose!

MOON: Pardon me, but that's my line. It's the prerogative of the one who jilts a woman also to insult her.

LARD: Of course, it would be a different story if you'd looked my daughter's way.

MOON: Do you think I'm not receptive to such charm?

LARD: I daresay, with Fritzi it would be an apple off a different tree. Your father's Excellency is just a title on a piece of paper, but with her . . . excellence is written all over her.

MOON: Divine Fritzi! While you're talking of her I feel how passion overwhelms me!

LARD: How fast you fall in love — your heart works like a revolving door!

MOON: Practice!

LARD: Now if we go about this right . . . Come on, let's talk about it a little more . . . (*Takes his arm.*)

MOON: I'm open to suggestions. As a former butcher you wouldn't give me a bum steer.

LARD (*intimately, while leaving with Moon*): My Fritzi, that's a morsel for a young Tchinelli, not the sister-in-law!

(*Both leave.*)

Scene 15

FERDINAND (*from back left*): Alfred will think I'm a louse — he'll believe that I'm after the money — I have to act fast to help him.

VINCELLI (*entering from background*): What's the delay? Lard promised to get the local priest . . .

FERDINAND (*stepping forward*): Your Excellency, I'm the one who's supposed to marry for money . . .

VINCELLI: Ah, just in time! (*Looking him over*) Well, I think the person can be quite satisfied with you.

FERDINAND: She has asked me to give this locket to Your Excellency. (*Hands Ulrike's locket to Vincelli.*)

VINCELLI: The renegade has probably given her his portrait — I'm glad to get it back . . . (*Opens the locket.*) Heavens, is it possible? (*In great emotion*) That's Amalia's picture . . . yes, yes, exactly . . . (*To Ferdinand*) How did she . . . (*Trying to collect himself*) Tell her, I will . . . (*Turning away to hide his emotions, then turning back to Ferdinand*) Tell her I'll compensate her amply for the picture, however it came into her possession. Here is the draft for the money I agreed to pay you for marrying . . .

FERDINAND (*mustering his courage*): I'm sorry, Your Excellency, but the bride no longer is for sale . . .

VINCELLI (*puzzled*): How so?

FERDINAND: Your son is already secretly married.

VINCELLI (*shocked*): How . . . ! What . . . !? Impossible!

FERDINAND: It's been nine days . . . last Wednesday.

VINCELLI (*wringing his hands*): Terrible . . . ! (*Overcome with anger*) Where is he that I can invoke my curse on . . .

Scene 16

LARD (*rushing with Moon from the background, to Ferdinand*): You're a liar!

MOON: Heaven is the witness of my bachelorhood! I'm unmarried . . . that's my only virtue!

LARD (*to Vincelli*): Tchinelli, take it from an expert: You're being sold a lot of tripe!

MOON (*to Ferdinand*): You found out . . . but that's no
way to get even . . .

VINCELLI (*to himself, amazed*): What do these people
want?

FERDINAND (*to Moon*): Found out? What?

MOON: That I made your ex-Fritzi believe that her father
was hidden in the room where . . .

FERDINAND: Where I was?!

MOON: Just a little trick to start trouble between the two
of you . . .

FERDINAND (*furiously*): Is that what you did . . . ?!

MOON: But that's no reason to estrange a father from his
son.

FERDINAND: Why, you dirty . . . ! (*Goes after Moon furiously.*)

MOON (*seeking refuge behind Vincelli*): Father, protect
your son!

LARD (*pushing Ferdinand back*): Servants! Help! Police!

VINCELLI (*extremely puzzled, pointing at Moon*): Is this
person drunk?

MOON: Yes, drunk with joy, with filial joy! Allow me to present myself as the consequence of Your Excellency's youthful slip.

VINCELLI: Will someone get this fellow off my back?

LARD: Shame, Tchinelli, don't be cruel. He's a good son, he
won't marry the sister-in-law, just as you wanted!

VINCELLI (*outraged*): To what vulgar jests am I exposed
here?

Scene 17

ALFRED (*from back, right*): Once more, Father, let me try
to change your . . .

VINCELLI: Out of my eyes, forever! The sight of you is painful to me!

ALFRED: How can you hate a son just because he loves an
angel?

VINCELLI: Angel? This is maddening! This trollop an angel!
Look here, you deluded dupe, this is how a girl must look
whom one can call an angel! (*Shows him the picture in
the locket.*) Such beauty could overcome differences in
rank, for such loveliness one might plead special consid-
erations . . .

ALFRED (*delighted*):   Father, I'll hold you to your word!
(*Runs off at right back.*)

LARD (*puzzled, to Vincelli*):   What? This is your son?

VINCELLI: Why yes, who else?

LARD: The secretary? (*To Moon*) What kind of a son are
you, then?

MOON: I'm a son who (*Pointing at Vincelli*) could urgently
use a father like him.

(*Alfred enters with Ulrike from background, right.
He leads her to Vincelli.*)

VINCELLI: What is that?

ALFRED: Such beauty, you just said, justifies special con-
sideration — so give your consent to me and my bride . . .

VINCELLI (*in utmost amazement, looking at Ulrike*):   This
is . . . it is she . . . in every feature she resembles . . .

ULRIKE (*pointing at the locket in Vincelli's hand*):   The picture of my mother as she looked when you loved her, before she was forced to become the wife of my father . . .

VINCELLI (*softly, embarrassed*):   Don't talk about it . . . I
have . . . ah, how this still affects me . . . the people will
notice . . .

ALFRED: Do you still hesitate to bless our union?

VINCELLI: But you already . . . well . . .

ALFRED: Tomorrow will be our wedding!

VINCELLI: How often do you want to get married?

ALFRED: What do you mean?

VINCELLI: Aren't you married yet?

ALFRED: How did you get that idea?

VINCELLI (*pointing to Ferdinand*):   This man here . . . (*To Alfred*) So . . . not married yet? Well, then I still have time . . .

ALFRED: . . . to join our hands with your blessing!

VINCELLI (*to himself*):   If only I could control my emotions . . . (*To Alfred*) All right, take her, you stubborn boy! (*Joins their hands.*)

ALFRED: Father! You make me happy beyond words!

VINCELLI (*softly to Alfred*):   The way I might have been, too, if I had been as stubborn as you are.

LARD (*to Moon*):   And to you, you wretch, I offered my daughter? If this gets around, the girl will be compromised for life! This is a nightmare . . . I have a compromised daughter!

MOON: For a couple of thousand thalers I promise discreet silence.

FERDINAND (*running toward right background where Fritzi comes on the stage*):   Fritzi!

FRITZI: Ferdinand!

LARD (*quickly making up his mind, to Ferdinand*):   Friend, you want her? Take her! Can a father be briefer? (*Joins their hands together.*)

LUCIA (*coming from left*):   The suit is filed for breach of promise.

LARD: Don't waste your money on a suit, the rascal is a fraud!

LUCIA: What?

MOON: A clever fish, you mean to say?

FERDINAND: Who, thank heavens, got caught in his own net. And that ought to happen to everyone who calls himself a clever fish just because he operates in cold blood.

MOON (*to Lucia*):   Is there no pardon in your heart for a soldier of fortune who went over the hill and came back to re-enlist?

LUCIA (*very angrily*):   Out of my sight!

MOON: I suppose even the brightest moon has an eclipse now and then. Well, I'd better go and see if the Inn-keeper's wife can get her husband to hire me as a waiter. (*To the other two couples*) We didn't do so badly here to-night. Out of three love affairs, two will end in wedding bells. That's about all you can expect in a farce with music — good luck, everybody! (*Exits.*)

LARD: A toast! Tchinelli! Long live the young couples!

(*The orchestra plays cheerful music as the curtain falls.*)